Praise for "HOLY CRAP

Jolene's words are an accurate reflection of the multiple roles women play in agriculture. I've laughed at her humorous and poignant stories and I've seen her open her arms to hug those needing a friend. *Holy Crap! I Married a Farmer!* is like having Jolene right next door.

– Sherry Saylor
American Farm Bureau Women's Leadership Committee Chair, Farmer
ARIZONA

If you are engaged to, newly married to, or been married to a farmer or rancher for years, this book has the sanity you need, are looking for, or thought you lost! *Holy Crap! I Married a Farmer!* is filled with laughter and tears from the heart of honesty. An absolute must read!

– Holly Marshall-Heber
Farm and Ranch Co-owner/Operator
SOUTH DAKOTA

Jolene's book, *Holy Crap! I Married a Farmer!* is a perfect gift to build stronger bonds between generations. Moms, daughters and in-laws will celebrate her warmth and wit as she shines the light on the dynamics of family relationships.

– Lora Kilgore-Norquest
Ag Women of the Heartland, Research Scientist at Pioneer Hi-Bred
KANSAS

Holy Crap! I Married a Farmer! is just what we men need to build a stronger partnership with our spouse. With honesty and humor, Jolene's understanding of relationships captures the special dynamics of our family farms.

– Shaun Haney
RealAgriculture
ALBERTA, CANADA

HOLY CRAP!
I MARRIED A FARMER!

Joy-filled Lessons Connecting
Our Sisters in Agriculture

BY
JOLENE BROWN
WITH SPECIAL CONTRIBUTIONS FROM CATHY RILEY

Published by Telemachus Press, LLC
www.Telemachuspress.com

ISBN# 978-1-945330-51-3

Library of Congress Control Number: 2017931666

HUMOR / Marriage & Family

Written by Jolene Brown

Special Contributions by Cathy Riley

Edited by Barbara McNichol Editorial

Designed by Matthew Eberhart

Illustrated by Charles Lockhart

Content used with permission:

Alison Bos – blogger at myAGventures.com (page 30)

Kathy Peterson – professional speaker at PeopleWorksInc.com (page 64)

Dr. Beverly Smallwood – licensed psychologist and author
of *This Wasn't Supposed to Happen to Me* (page 102)

DEDICATION

This book is dedicated to my Sisters in Agriculture who are or have been actively involved on the farm and connected to those wonderfully crazy farmers. Thank you for your voluntary and anonymous contributions filled with real life wisdom and fun. For years we have shared laughter, tears, and cheers.

I also dedicate this to my real life sisters, Sherami and Carmelee. We've traversed quite a journey together. Your love and support never waiver.

Without Cathy Riley, this book would not exist. Her belief in the purpose of this book, and the hours we spent together organizing, brainstorming, and writing were hours of great joy and oh so much laughter.

And especially, this book is dedicated to my husband, Keith, and our two daughters, Callista and Miranda. You were and are the very best teachers to this student. Thank you for your love.

A NOTE FROM JOLENE

"No way."
"I will never marry a farmer!"
"It's the last thing I'd ever do."

These exact words are often spoken when a woman expresses her dreams for a future spouse. They're adamant and concise; no farmer; no way.

If this describers you, perhaps this opinion was formed because you were raised on a farm and experienced the demands of the business and lifestyle of agriculture. Perhaps you happily have a full-time job or career in a city or town. Perhaps you've never set foot on a farm and have no desire to do so. When talking to your friends or family, you're clear, "I will never marry a farmer!"

Then Cupid strikes. Before you know it, a ring shines on your finger. In spite of declaring "no way," you said, "I do."

You've done the inevitable; you've married a farmer. Or even more challenging, you've become two farmers married to each other. You find yourself living in the midst of Mother Nature's whims, financial pressures, seasonal "personality disorder," multiple involved family members, and feelings of isolation. At times you wonder, "Is anyone else going through this?"

Know this to be true: *You are NOT alone.*

The life-changing event of marrying a farmer requires new learning, adaptation, collaboration, leadership, management, labor, laughter, and love. It opens you to a world of challenge and celebration. But marrying a farmer goes far beyond the traditional "getting used to being a couple" and "having a job." Farm life incorporates the business and the family, the lifestyle and the living.

I've been married to a farmer for more than four decades and have learned it's not wise to travel this journey alone. The days and years become easier with the help of others—family, friends, peers, and new connections. That's why hundreds of Sisters in Agriculture have willingly shared their fun-filled spirits and life lessons. Their words of wisdom came through conferences, e-mails, phone calls, and personal conversations. Throughout this book you'll read insightful stories and tips from me, contributor Cathy Riley, and several of our Sisters in Agriculture.

Let this book be your companion and your roadmap. It offers you hope and help, laughter while you learn, and dozens of reasons to celebrate because—Holy Crap! You did marry a farmer!

Jolene

TABLE OF CONTENTS

CHAPTER 1

"Honey, got a minute?"

AGRICULTURE HAS ITS OWN CLOCK

Honey, got a minute? As a woman connected to the farm, you'll find it necessary to define and honor your choices of how to spend your time. It may not be the same as your spouse, mother, or mother-in-law strongly suggests, but it's important you do what's important to you both on and off the farm.

Jolene's Experience

During my husband's growing-up years, he was privileged to always have a daily selection of amazing homemade breads. My mother-in-law could mix, knead, and bake a batch of her special breads and rolls with gusto and ease. As a new daughter-in-law with little bread-baking experience, I became an avid student. I asked for her recipes and began to learn.

> It's important you do what's important to you.

That's when I found out that a "tablespoon" meant the size of the largest tablespoon in the silverware drawer, not a measuring spoon; that potato water was saved from the meal before and used in making the dough; that "knead until it feels right" requires a lot of experience; that "bake until golden brown" is not a specific time but a test of the color of the bottom of the loaf of bread and how it sounds when you "thump" the top; that her recipe made seven large loaves—a big batch for a beginner.

But begin I did. I measured, mixed, kneaded, and then placed a beautiful big batch of dough in my greased roaster pan. I set the pan to rise in the gas oven. (The pilot light keeps it at just the right temperature to rise properly.) Of course, it was during one of those "rising times" that my husband stuck his head in the kitchen door and shouted, "Honey, got a minute? The cattle are in the corn field, and we need someone at the gate."

I grabbed my coat, pulled on my boots, and ran out the door. It was hours later—with cattle returned safely to the lot, boots off, and coat back on the hook—that I remembered. THE BREAD!

After opening the oven door, I found the risen yeast dough had popped the lid, run over the side, slithered through two oven racks, and made its way through the bottom oven vents to puddle on the heating element. A mess for sure!

If only I had known what "Honey, got a minute?" really meant, I would have put the dough in the refrigerator before heading out the door.

You'll find there are short cuts and things that take much longer. There are times of crisis and times that really could wait "a minute." So when faced with a frantic, urgent situation, I've learned to quickly ask myself, "Does this involve blood, guts, and gore? And if there is no action right now, will there be damage to life or property?" If my answer to either question is "Yes!" you can bet I'm on the move. If my answer is "No" to both of those questions, I take a deep breath. Hopefully my response might come from a place of reason rather than a framing of disaster. (By the way, cows on the road? Run. Cows in the corn field? Breathe, quickly put bread in refrigerator, run.)

Insights from Our Sisters in Agriculture

- When you hear the request, "Honey, got a minute?" it means right this minute someone needs help. So turn off all appliances, bring to a halt everything you're doing, make sure the kids are safe, and dress for the weather, knowing you'll be gone much longer than "a minute." You might be home by bedtime. Maybe.

"Got a minute?" never means a minute.

- I love it when he hands you his shopping list and, before you've even left home, he asks, "When will you be back?" Best to never tell him you're going to town!

- I have a great college education, but it did not include how to move livestock, use a wrench, fill the planter, run the grain cart, load trucks by eye-balling the correct amount of corn or beans, help with the birth of a calf, say good-bye to a sick animal, talk with our banker, advocate for agriculture—and all the while, keep up with family needs. Know what's interesting? When my spouse sees me sitting down for five minutes, he asks, "What are you doing?"

There's your time, his time, and family time. And they're all influenced by farm time set by Mother Nature's seasons.

There's field time: preparation, planting, scouting, protecting, harvesting. There are times that include when the soil is dry enough, when it's moist enough, before the ground freezes, after the frost goes out, before it rains, after it rains, and when it never rains.

There's animal time: breeding, feeding, birthing, health monitoring, and daily caring for newborns through their stages of growth.

There's equipment time: buying and selling it, learning to operate it, operating it, and repairing it.

There's property time: mowing, repairing, replacing, removing snow, and building new structures.

There's finance time: marketing, buying, selling, analyzing, monitoring cash flow and net worth, taxes, borrowing, leasing, renting, owning, and getting paid—or not.

There's leadership and management time: visioning, goal-setting, business planning, hiring, coaching, evaluating, firing, protecting risk, complying with regulations, doing public relations, and giving back to the community and industry. It's also a non-stop job using our time to productively and positively create change.

All of these require continuing education time. Four major factors— pace, perceptions, process, and products—influence time on our farms, and each one is changing in these ways:

1.) The pace has accelerated for farmers to make decisions, to adapt and use technology, to increase production and complete the work.

2.) The perceptions of agriculture have changed from one of trust to one of questioning how we work. That means more time is needed for education and farm advocacy.

3.) The process of how we farm requires more record keeping, monitoring, reporting, and showing the results of our daily activities than ever before.

4.) The products we market are changing as we strive to meet our customers' needs while working through increasing numbers of rules and regulations.

Timing in agriculture is not set by a clock, nor do we work from nine to five. The hours are long, the work demanding and diverse. Yet, we all receive those phone calls indicating our work is not perceived as work. We hear, "Since you don't have a job, I bet you have time to volunteer for . . ."

Yes, our jobs on the farm are real jobs and 24 hours in a day is all we get—no more, no less. That's why we must be intentional with our goals and priorities. Certainly, desired opportunities to volunteer, lead, and serve come our way. And yes, we Sisters in Agriculture are among the best at managing multiple roles.

> Timing in agriculture is not set by a clock.

But remember, when expectations and choices meet the reality of limited time, you have to take care of you. That's best done by saying either "yes" or "no." An effective way to say "no" might be as direct as this: "I'm sorry, my answer has to be 'no' and please don't ask me why." Then steer inquirers to a resource or quickly change the subject. If they ask again in a different way, give the same response.

Most important, don't change these words: "I'm sorry, my answer has to be 'no.'" It's futile to justify your reasons, so don't!

To build a foundation for deciding how to spend your time, ask these three beginning questions:

- **How is my health?** (physical, mental, spiritual)
- **How are my relationships?** (relationships with those important to you and with those who need you)
- **How well am I completing items on my "bucket list"?** (things we still want to experience, have, be, feel, or become)

Managing your time so you can take care of you is the best gift you can give yourself—and others. ❖

CHAPTER 2

"Mealtime—whenever, wherever, whomever"

FOOD AND FLEXIBILITY

Everyone who prepares and serves meals for her farm family has to negotiate a whole bunch of expectations. Few women in agriculture are privileged to have meals via home delivery or ones you can pick up prepared on their way home unless they live close to town. "Fast food" on the farm means you've already prepared the meals and stored them in the freezer. Still, you'd like to open the refrigerator door wishing a beautiful meal would miraculously appear.

> "fast food" means you've already prepared the meals.

There are many choices of meals you may offer and who prepares it. Your preferences and standards will become clear as you negotiate your own needs as well as the needs of those you love and serve.

Most farm families find that during the peak times of farm work, it's not uncommon to eat in shifts—that is, feed the kids first and then feed the

farm workers whenever they show up. But don't forget to feed you! Others tell of late nights when everyone is just too tired to prepare a meal and even too tired to eat. More than once a woman has said to her fatigued farmer, "I just wish I could put this nourishment in an IV so you wouldn't have to muster up the energy to get the fork to your mouth."

Mealtime is wherever the mouths may be.

Jolene's Experience

I'll never forget a young daughter-in-law I met at a Women in Agriculture Conference who talked about different mealtime standards. She said that after a full day's work, she knew her father-in-law returned home for an evening meal of pot roast, carrots, potatoes, apple salad, muffins, and cake. Those nights, though, she and her husband had popcorn for supper. In each case, both spouses were happy.

Insights from Our Sisters in Agriculture

- Mealtime is wherever the mouths may be. This includes a tractor cab, pickup tailgate, carpentry shop, picnic table, blanket on the ground, or the kitchen table. Who prepares it, how it's served, and time of day are all subject to change.

- I prepare the evening meal to be served at 6 p.m. at the kitchen table. If anyone wants food, that's where and when it is. If they need it at a later time, they can warm it up themselves.

- Keep reusable bottles filled with water in the freezer. They can be used as an ice pack, body temp cooler, or thirst quencher. Dehydration can happen quickly during hot, long, work-filled days. Lack of water makes for a grumpy farmer!

- Setting a mealtime standard took a bit of "training" because previous generations had different models. For months, my father-in-law struggled when his son (my husband) left the field to go home to eat, and then returned about an hour later. Now, it just happens.

- If they show up in the yard for a meal and it isn't quite ready, set the table quickly. They'll know the meal is soon on the way.

- During harvest, throw food at them, keep walking, and do not make eye contact!

- Crockpots are a farm meal preparer's best friend. Don't forget to ask your friends and neighbors for crockpot recipes.

- A new daughter-in-law shared, Be careful if you put a "racy" note in your new husband's lunchbox and place it in his pick-up. I soon discovered that, on this farm, not only do the men exchange vehicles, they exchange lunch boxes. My father-in-law will never look at me the same!

- Don't complete final meal prep and especially don't dish up until you see the whites of their eyes.

- In the fall, you can toss food at them like you're at the zoo. There are many busy, busy days and nights when it feels like you are living in a zoo, full of crazy, wild, demanding animals.

Other "peak times" increase the need for mealtime flexibility, especially as children grow. With school demands, farm chores, and extra-curricular activities, you'll find yourself traveling many a gravel road over long distances to a location others take for granted. And because you are rural, you may have few options for carpooling. Shift-eating and packing food may be the norm for your children on the go.

Jolene's Experience

Our two daughters were very involved in sports, music, theater, and more so we parents spent a lot of time on the bleachers. I clearly remember one evening when my husband came running up the basement steps, still toweling his hair after a fast shower. He looked into the kitchen, saw the table set for four, and said, "You mean we don't have to be somewhere?"

Insights from Our Sisters in Agriculture

- Farmers give new meaning to "meals on wheels." If you think supper delivered to the field will be one stop . . . think again. Workers in different fields sometimes expect to eat while waiting in line at the co-op elevator. So bring an ice chest and a way to keep things warm. Also bring your e-reader or a book or magazine. You can predict they'll never be on your end of the field when you deliver the food.

> The food will not magically appear!

- During peak times (planting, harvesting, calving, farrowing, etc.), reduce the number of spicy foods you serve. It upsets the stomach and the personalities.

- During harvest my husband runs the combine and I run the grain cart. At lunch time I love it when he says, "What's for lunch today?" Of course my response is, "I'll check with the cook when I see her."

- My husband called me on the phone and said, "Hi honey. You'll need to add a little more water to the soup." (That means he's just invited three people to join us for lunch.) I told him, "I'm not making soup." He replied, "I bet you'll figure something out. See you in ten minutes." That's why microwaves were invented and we keep dinner options in the freezer.

- I love it when our son's friend comes over and asks, "What's in the grocery store today?" He knows we live 40 minutes from the closest store so we'd better have things well stocked in the farm's pantry and freezer—aka "grocery store.'"

There's no right or wrong way to do mealtime. Figure out what works for you today and it may need to change tomorrow. Most of all, be sure to celebrate when you've set a routine schedule and the whole family can be at the same meal table at the same time. While our bodies are being nourished, we have fun catching up, sharing laughs, and looking into the eyes of each family member with affection.

———————————

Mealtime is also an excellent time to remember how blessed we are to live in a country in which we have a choice of the foods we prepare, offer, and eat. Let's treasure "breaking bread" together—whenever, wherever, with whomever. ✤

CHAPTER 3

"If things are not OK at home, things are not OK."

CONNECTING WITH FAMILY

It's the important people in our lives who can give us the most joy or pain—and the most satisfaction or frustration. With the multitude of demands on the farm, being intentional in interacting with family members has a big effect. Being present in a family requires a time commitment to focus on each other, individually and as a unit. This allows us to experience life more cohesively with support from and for each other.

Yet we so often forget to connect the value in our daily work to the important people in our world. We can forget that work can wait.

Remember that building special relationships often happens while riding along in the combine, driving to a farm show, sorting hogs, picking vegetables, driving children to activities, snuggling with a toddler, recognizing accomplishments, and holding someone with a hurting heart in your arms. It happens, too, as you tuck your little one into bed, compliment your teenager, or hold your spouse's hand as you say your evening prayers.

> Connect the value
> of our work to
> the people
> in our world.

Jolene's Experience

During the winter of my first pregnancy, I embroidered what I thought was a piece of art but discovered it was actually a piece of philosophy. The words still resonate today: "Cleaning and scrubbing can wait till tomorrow for babies grow up, we learn to our sorrow. So quiet down cobwebs and dust go to sleep. I'm rocking my babies and babies don't keep."

Cathy's Experience

I didn't know how lonely my mother may have been as the woman on the farm. Oh, her days were busy—six children to care for, long days of spring planting, and endless hours of harvest that made her a single parent every year. In many ways, she really was a single parent shuffling kids from little league baseball games, to and from piano lessons, 4-H meetings, and so much more. And she made it look so easy. The quick and often rushed conversations with my father were about an equipment part, the weather forecast, the markets, or the errands she needed to run. What kept her going when her shoulders carried so much of the load? Was she really appreciated? Is that why faith was the foundation of her life?

> Mom was
> never alone.
> She had God.

Today, I look at Mom's journey and realize she was never ever really alone. She had God.

Insights from Our Sisters in Agriculture

- In the deep dark of the night, it's not the number of acres you own, the color of equipment you have, or the pedigrees of your cow herd that matter. In the deep dark of the night, it's the people you've touched, helped, led, and held that give meaning to your life.

- If your children have an education, talents, goals, and a special relationship that take them away from the farm, let them go—without guilt. Our son wanted to farm on his own and we supported his decision. Our daughter moved across the country. Were those our goals? No. Their goals? Yes. We are still connected as a family because we let go.

> Children are to fulfill their dreams not ours.

- None of our children are interested in farming. One wants to be a dentist, another an accountant, another a massage therapist. We must understand that their role in life is to fulfill their own dreams, not ours.

- Our son farmed with us for seven years. Then he met and married the woman of his heart. Her job was hours away, and she wanted to continue her career. Commuting for our son to the farm wasn't possible. As much as we wanted him to stay, naturally he wanted to go and be with her, so we didn't make our relationship an "either/or" proposition. We honored his decision. He found a job he loves in her location and uses his vacation days to return and help us plant and harvest. And today, we are happily welcomed into their home and into the lives of our grandchildren.

Jolene's Experience

My phone has rung many a time with a young farm or ranch woman on the other end asking, "Is this really how it is?" Each woman has concerns such as these: "One moment I was doing the important work on the farm—driving the combine, meeting with suppliers, talking with our loan officer, making marketing decisions, and attending a local farm or ag education event. My work and contribution were acknowledged by my husband, his family, and even the community. Now my days are filled with caring for babies and small children—feeding, laundry, diapers, runny noses, toys everywhere, and very few coordinated nap times. Sometimes the tears are not just theirs. I know raising children is the most important work I can do, but why don't those around me regard it as important as the work of the farm? And sometimes I wonder if I myself haven't really accepted that raising kids is the most important work on the farm."

> Raising children is the most important job on the farm.

Raising Kids on a Farm

Whether it's through osmosis or intentional experiences, the education of a child raised on a farm comes with its own curriculum. Alison Bos, a Missouri friend and great blogger at myAGventures.com, sums it up with these points:

> We felt like the luckiest kids alive.

My brother and I had our chore clothes, and before going outside, we needed to change from our "good" clothes. From a young age, we learned that experience was a great teacher. We also learned if we get stuck in the mud with our boots on, we'd better just stay put and wait for help.

We learned that when Mom or Dad said the electric fence was "hot," they weren't kidding—and it had nothing to do with the outside temperature.

We learned how to climb through barb wire fences without getting scratched or our clothes torn.

We learned how to hold the bottle while feeding a baby calf. For me, bottle feeding a baby animal was so much better than playing house!

We had rules to follow when playing outside. My favorite: Don't go near the bull!

We understood that if we opened a gate, we'd better shut it.

We learned the worst form of punishment was being sent to the house and not being allowed to play outside.

Being chased by a chicken, bucked off a horse, or

falling out of a tree didn't slow us down one bit.

What seemed like work to some kids was fun for me—such as picking up rocks in the fields with a stoneboat. We called it a Rock Party.

We didn't eat our night meal until the chores were done. And we didn't complain about it.

Bonding time with Dad was best when he worked out in the field. Sometimes we got to sit on his lap in the combine (although today we'd be in a buddy seat). We got to go around and around the field planting corn or baling hay, seriously feeling like the luckiest kids alive.

Growing up on the farm meant the best meals ever. Mom cooked everything herself. She was also the best nurse, making our bumps, scrapes, and bruises go away. She could get manure and mud stains out of our "good" clothes that we shouldn't have worn for play or farm work. She would go run a tractor, haul the pigs or beef cattle to market, tend to the sick animals, stay up all night long in the farrowing house delivering

baby pigs, and she could back up a trailer just as good (sometimes better) than Dad.

Yes, we had swings and sand boxes, but those were nothing compared to playing in the hay mow, talking to baby animals, or throwing rocks in a puddle. Now that was fun!

We learned the cycle of life.

Well before we could legally drive a car, we were driving tractors and farm trucks, first around the farmstead and then in the fields.

As farm kids, we saw more live animal births than any of our classmates. Sadly, we've also seen births that did not end well—another lesson in the cycle of life.

We had manners and learned to respect our elders. We learned to listen and follow instructions and earn the right for fun.

For schoolwork, a lot of our assignments or projects incorporated farming into them. My biology project was dissecting a pig and identifying its parts.

We had that one animal—a dog, cat, or horse—that was a buddy and best friend. We also learned that not all animals on the farm are pets.

We were proud to be members of 4-H and FFA.

No Christmas list was complete without those farm sets, more toy tractors, wagons, trucks, and balers. We had plastic pigs, horses, cows, and hay bales. We used real shelled corn from the harvest, and we needed more of these sets each Christmas to make the farm "bigger." I still have some of these toys.

The older we got, the more responsibilities and chores we were given. No, we were not slaves. We weren't overworked. Our parents were teaching us one of the most important lessons—responsibility. They believed in this comment by Abigail Van Buren (Dear Abby): "If you want children to keep their feet on the ground, put some responsibility on their shoulders."

The farm raised me.

Oh what a gift to be raised on a farm. Thanks, Mom and Dad!

Jolene's Experience

Many say, "I was raised on a farm." But I say, "The farm raised me." From sun up to sun down, through all the seasons of the year, the "curriculum" continues to this day. And I wouldn't change that education for anything. Many of these lessons I learned might apply to you:

We learn the importance of "neighboring"—that is, helping others and asking for their help. And you don't expect or exchange money.

We learn that bottle feeding baby animals and snitching fresh garden peas is so much more fun than any video game.

We learn that a place for nap time may be on pillows behind the tractor seat. It's easy to go to sleep lying down and seeing row after row after row out the back window.

We learn the mail carrier appreciates stopping by our mail box, the usual red flag up, only to find a homemade treat just for him.

We learn the joy of delivering violets in a May basket and hanging it as a surprise on our neighbor's door knob.

We learn that if Mom picks us up from school with a big snack, we're riding along while she goes a distance after equipment parts.

We learn the very best place to trick-or-treat on Halloween is at the home of our rural neighbors. At each stop, we're greeted with food treats, trinkets, art supplies, small toys, and more. Of course, Mom called earlier to ask if they'll be home, if they'd welcome a trick-or-treater, and what time is best to arrive.

We learn that two of the most important people in our lives are the weatherman and the person who gets the electricity flowing again.

Nothing beats hands-on learning.

We learn that our town friends love to come and spend days with us at the farm. But some of our friends' parents prefer not to drive on gravel roads, so if we want to play with them, it's Mom who picks them up and takes them home. And to her, it's no big deal.

We learn that working or playing on the farm, we will get dirty. We have to clean up a bit before coming into the house and clean up a lot before visiting someone else or going into town.

We learn about life and death and how babies are made.

We learn that safety must come before turning a key, being around animals, or working on equipment. Our parents made sure we knew the consequences if we ignored the steps to staying safe. Safe practices were not optional!

We learn about things we can control and things we can't. But we never look for someone else to blame.

We learn that working on a farm includes real exercise that requires us to be in shape. We know we'll be physically tired at night.

We learn that Mother Nature trumps all plans. Months of work (and large investments) can be lost in a single storm. Our home and other buildings can be swept downstream in a flood or blown away in a tornado.

We know our neighbors will be the first to offer to help, and they'll be around for as long as it takes.

We learn the value of a work ethic and showing up on time. Sometimes we get paid; most of the time we don't. But we know something or someone is depending on us, so we just do it.

Cathy's Experience

I was once told by the boss of my then 22-year-old son that he knew right away my son came from a farm. The employer said, "On his first day at work, he arrived ready to go about twenty minutes before start time. And he continues to be the first one at work each day."

> Being bored
> is not
> acceptable.

Children on the farm don't understand the meaning of phrases such as "passing the time" or "just keeping busy." Being bored is not acceptable when you have space and land, animals and machines, wood and wire, trees and creeks, tools and time. Many of the children's friends visiting the farm just haven't figured that out.

Not long ago, our nephew, a town boy, wanted to spend time with us on the farm. He arrived with a big smile on his face and his Game Boy in hand, expecting he'd have plenty of time to play when the farm work got done. Not so!

Children who grow up on a farm use a lot of technology and see their parents applying its use in every aspect of today's farm work. Complex technology is interwoven in nearly every piece of today's farm equipment and crop and animal management. Oh yes, on the farm, children are also surrounded by smart phones, iPads, computers, games, and plenty

of options for "screen time." But unlike my nephew, they have learned the time and place for each use.

———————————

The seasons of the year and our work on the farm give us a structure. They also give us the freedom and opportunity to spend time around family. Bonds are formed through mutual goals—to live on the farm, do the work, learn from each other, support each other, and love each other. Then no matter where we go in our lives, "if things are OK at home, things are OK." ❖

CHAPTER 4

"Oh what a tangled web we weave!"

COMPLEXITIES OF FAMILY RELATIONSHIPS

The logistics of farming mean you'll probably be "neighbors" to family including parents, grandparents, siblings, in-laws, and more. Although we recommend you should never live within a binocular's view of another family member, sometimes practicality gets in the way and physical boundaries become blurred. We go to each other's houses for family gatherings; our children play together; the adults work together and see each other almost every day. The web can get tangled, requiring careful attention to needs as well as ways to deal with conflict, boundaries, and differing goals.

> Never live within a binocular's view of another family member.

Advice for Daughters-in-law

When it comes to doing farm jobs, many a young bride has been advised by her mother-in-law, "Do not learn how to do something on the farm if you don't want to do it the rest of your life. It often becomes your job from that day forward."

A similar lesson was shared by a quick-learning daughter-in-law who said, "If you do something badly enough, you won't be asked to do it again!"

If you want to know how your spouse will respect you, observe how he treats his mother. If you can, spend time with your future in-laws before you marry. Make sure you like his parents. If you don't, you will have a whole bunch of stories to tell later, and they won't be happy ones.

> Do not try to compete with the radio broadcaster. You probably won't win.

You'll quickly learn about two areas on the farm of vital importance—the weather and the markets. Do not try to compete for his attention while the radio broadcaster gives those reports. You probably won't win. Instead, you'll hear:

"Shhhhhhh . . . the weather's on." Did it rain? How much rain? Did they get rain? Praying for rain. Praying for no rain. Check the radar. What's the temperature? What's the wind speed? How much snow? Is the back-up generator working?

"Shhhhhhh . . . the markets are on." You'll be asked to understand basis, cash markets, options, hedging, margins, longs or shorts, nearby futures, puts and calls, and more. And above all else, when a major farm commodity report is being announced, be quiet!

Jolene's Experience

A young woman once asked me, "How long do you have to be married before you get to be family?" I could not speak to the complexities of her situation, but I did say, "If you were my daughter-in-law, the minute that ring was placed on your finger, you became family, my daughter. I believe it's my job to do all I can to support you and your marriage—to respect your work, your home, your heart. I would like to find out what's important to you. I'd help if you would ask, but I don't want to interfere. And I need to make sure I thank you because you are the one who puts the twinkle in my son's eyes. The joy you bring him is joy you bring to this whole family."

I continued, "Now, if you're asking what it takes to be part of a family business, then we'd have a business meeting to get you up to speed on what's required for any potential employee to work in this business. And if you need security or understanding of your husband's roles and responsibilities, the two of you can have a family business conversation with us. We want to make sure you feel welcomed, respected, and informed."

Cathy's Experience

We had just returned from our honeymoon and, within a few minutes, my husband of five days informed me he was heading to the field to plant soybeans. I watched him walk down the sidewalk and drive away in his truck, knowing I was no longer his number one priority that day.

I called my mom and cried, "Mom, he's in the field, and I'm all alone. Now what do I do?" My mother's response took me by surprise. "You knew what you were getting into when you married a farmer. Make him a baloney sandwich and go ride along with him in the tractor." She taught me right then about going to him when he couldn't come to me. It's advice I'd give to any new farmer's wife.

Insights from Our Sisters in Agriculture

- You will learn to identify equipment and vehicles by sounds—the combine, the skid-steer loader, the big tractor, the four-wheeler, the semi-truck, the pick-up truck. And you will need to know because it's the first clue about where you might find your husband.

- Remember, even if you have bought the farm land and buildings from the senior generation, it's still "their farm."

> Farmers become very good farmers once they quit farming.

- Farmers (and in-laws) become very good farmers once they quit farming.

- Just because your in-laws may live close to you doesn't mean they are always available to babysit. They probably don't expect to be paid, but they do deserve the respect of you asking first. And understand if they say "no."

- Be ready. Nothing prepares a new wife for the time she walks through a Co-Op elevator's doorway and finds a group of men sitting around the counter talking and drinking morning coffee, then it suddenly becomes deathly quiet. Bring brownies with you; it breaks the ice and they welcome you in.

- Be sure you know who you're talking to on the phone. I was expecting a call back from my husband so I quickly answered, "Hi, you sexy big hunk!" After a few moments of silence, my brother-in-law replied, "Thank you." Remember, private conversations and communications may not be so private on the farm.

- Don't worry about your mother-in-law running her finger over the furniture to find dust. When she lived there, there was dust, too.

- I've learned that when you move to the "home place" to be close to the farm work and your in-laws downsize into a new home, the "home place" is still their home. And all of your husband's siblings may have opinions about any changes you might make to their "growing-up home." Also, since you occupy the "home place," you may be the one expected to host the holiday gatherings. Set your boundaries early.

- If you don't agree with your in-laws or have questions, learn to speak up in the beginning. It may be too late if a decision has been made or a tradition has been established.

- The best gift I receive every year is a round-trip ticket to go back East and visit my family. This is purchased by my in-laws—not to get rid of me but to show they understand how much I miss my family. This is not my birthday or Christmas gift, but a gift just because they value me.

- When we were expecting our third child, we moved into my in-laws' old home. I knew it was hard for my father-in-law to leave the "home place" that was once his. After a month, he finally came out to talk with my husband while I was in the basement taking a shower. Since I was in the habit of running up the stairs without my clothes on, imagine my surprise when I rounded the corner and met my father-in-law face to face. He turned and quickly left the house. It took him another month before he came out to see us again.

> When I was your age, I had to walk three miles to school, uphill both ways!

- You'll hear a lot about "the good old days" and how hard things were back then. You'll hear, "When I was your age, I had to walk three miles to school, uphill both ways!" It's best if you just learn to nod your head and agree.

Advice for Mothers-in-law

One of the best gifts you can give your adult children when they marry is a "No Trespassing" sign for their yard. This means you promise to call before visiting and, if there are grandchildren, you may call a little more often.

Understand the importance of respecting your son's choice of whom he loves. And respect her for her choice of an occupation. Remember, her work is important to her; she's important to your son; your son's important to you; therefore, her work is important to you. Let your daughter-in-law bring wonderful, new perspectives to the things you do every day. And remember, just because you've always done something one way doesn't mean it's the only way.

Your daughter-in-law may be the one who finally tells you that you've done enough. How wonderful to have her on your team! I've heard many mothers-in-law openly say things such as, "She's the daughter I always wanted." I've heard many daughters-in-law openly say, "My mother-in-law is the best!" I've heard both in-laws share, "I'm so lucky to have her as family and in my life."

I also know getting to that place in an in-law relationship involves listening, respecting, laughing, crying, celebrating, appreciating, and at times biting your tongue. It's worth the investment.

> Just because you've always done something one way doesn't mean it's the only way.

Wouldn't it be better to look for better options and for the positives? Recently I sat on a park bench with a grandmother and her daughter-in-law watching the little ones play. My grandma friend turned to her daughter-in-law and said, "You are such a great mama to our grandchildren. You must be so tired at times with three little ones. Yet I love the way you play with them, and you are so patient. They certainly know they are loved." I just wish you could have seen her daughter-in-law's beaming face in that moment.

I received a call from a mother-in-law just furious because her son had recently married and they were going to "her family" for Christmas Eve. "Doesn't she know we always have family Christmas Eve here?" Then she exclaimed, "Well, if they don't come here Christmas Eve, they don't need to come at all. I bet your kids come to your house for your celebration!"

I asked her to breathe deeply and told her she probably wouldn't like what I had to say. "Whenever they come, it's a celebration, and I'm grateful. It may be on a holiday or before or after, or another season. But I'm glad they want to come. If you issue an ultimatum, you may start a battle that builds into a war. And never place your son into a position of choosing between his new bride and you. You may not win."

In general, let me say this: Mothers-in-law, when your adult children marry, a new family unit is started. This means new and old traditions may need to be considered, so take a breath and look at this situation from a new perspective.

Jolene's Experience

My father-in-law was still driving well into his early 90s. Most trips were out to the farm to "check on things," especially at planting and harvest. During an especially wet stretch in the spring, he drove into the driveway honking the horn. I hustled out to meet him and, with his car window down, a brief conversation followed.

Dad: *"Is he out planting corn today?"*
Me: *"No, Dad. We had four inches of rain last night. It's too wet."*
Dad: *"Well, you better tell him, it ain't gonna grow in the bag!"*
Me: *"I'll be sure to tell him that, Dad."*

Then he turned the car and drove out the driveway. (And no, I did not give that message to my busy husband.)

Cathy's Experience

Early in our marriage, I learned it's better to stifle the giggles and walk away. It had been a tough day in the field with seemingly endless equipment breakdowns. My father-in-law had just returned from the field with the next problem—a tractor repair. He had crawled underneath to begin work as my husband and I, having finished hog chores, asked if we could help. My father-in-law stopped long enough to give us both a disgusted look and yelled, "Turn off the radio."

"Turn off the radio?" my husband repeated. My father-in-law looked up from underneath the tractor and said, "Yes, turn off the radio, so I can see what I'm doing down here." Yup, it was time to stifle the giggles. We both knew better than to correct him. Besides, he wouldn't have thought it was as funny as we did.

Insights from Our Sisters in Agriculture

- Mother-in-law, be nice to your daughter-in-law for she is the one who will remember your birthday.

- I am forever grateful to my mother-in-law who taught me how not to treat my daughter-in-law.

- Be generous with deserved praise for your daughter-in-law. It costs little to speak the positive truth and it can mean so much.

- Now that my son is married, I receive the greatest gifts for Christmas and for my birthday. I know exactly who cared enough to thoughtfully pick them out. It quite obviously was not my son, but my daughter-in-law. I always make sure I thank her!

Mind the Generation Gap

When you become members of a farming team, you are no longer independent; you are interdependent. That sets up a need to ask, "What do you and your generation bring to the family and business? What do other generations bring? Why do they need you? Why do you need them?"

> Building on the strength of each generation is the goal.

Building on the strengths of each generation is the goal, yet each one has its challenges. Sometimes you just need to sit back and enjoy the interaction.

One of the best gifts adult children can give their parents while visiting their "growing-up home" is to realize they, the younger generation, may need to change their behaviors, especially their habits. One mother shared, "I aim to respect their boundaries, but what about mine? So many times my adult children walk into my home, open the refrigerator, take whatever they want, change the TV channel, and borrow without asking. Yes, I may offer all of those things, but couldn't they just ask?"

Jolene's Experience

I moderated a panel discussion of generations working together in which several in-laws were represented. As I concluded the session, I asked each panel member to offer a final word of advice. A wise mother-in-law shared, "Once a month I take my two daughters-in-law out for lunch. I pay for the meal and for childcare for our grandchildren. We go to a nice restaurant of their choice. During that time, I ask them about their jobs, hobbies, friends, and family. I know they gave up proximity to their family and friends to live here on the farm and become part of our family. I want to appreciate them and let them know I really care about them. And an added benefit happens when the three of us try to figure out how to get our three crazy husbands working together better."

I wish you could have seen the response from many in attendance. With wistful expressions, I could almost hear them sigh, "I want you for my mother-in-law!"

Cathy's Experience

Shortly after our oldest son graduated from college and returned to farm with us, it hit me. My husband and I had become our parents, dragging our feet when new ideas were proposed. And this time, it was our son excitedly talking about and proposing a purchase of new technology. As a member of the Millennial/digital generation, our son had done extensive research. He was convinced this piece would greatly benefit our farming operation. We older and wiser parents immediately dismissed the suggestion, having decided the technology couldn't possibly make us any money. Our son was naturally disappointed with our decision, but because he was sold on it, he purchased the technology on his own and installed it in his tractor. Oh yes, he did prove he was right, and we were wrong. Not only did it save the farm money, it was also good for the environment.

Insights from Our Sisters in Agriculture

- No matter where you live, you can't take the farm out of the farmer.

- Grandparents, remember you are not the parents of your grandchildren.

Respect: the foundation for healthy relationships.

- Be very frugal with advice, and it's best to offer it only when asked.

- A woman shared this about her 101-year-old father who lives in a nursing home and still listens to the weather. "He often calls the farm with specific directions: Be sure to put the snow blower on the tractor because we're going to get thirteen inches of snow today." We love his need and desire to still take care of things on the farm.

- I've learned to ask the younger generation to help me or answer my questions. They're more patient with me than my husband!

- As we're driving down the country road, daughter and grandchildren in the back seat, my farmer husband commented, "You see that field?

That tall stuff sticking up is water hemp. Just one plant can have up to 250,000 seeds. If that farmer lets that weed get out of hand, it will be a major problem for many years ahead, and he's losing money because it will affect his yield." Then he added, "Before you ever consider renting any farm ground to someone else, drive by their fields and farmsteads. If you see a mess like this, find a better farmer to be in business with." I call that windshield education.

- I remember driving home from church with my mom and dad only to have Dad stop by the side of the gravel road. Even though he was dressed in his Sunday best, he took time to pick mustard out of a neighbor's wheat field. His philosophy: "Take care of problems when they're small so they don't spread misery later." Guess he was teaching us much more than a lesson about farming.

- My father, age 90, still likes to run the combine for a little bit each year. Last year we used a forklift to get him to the platform so he could enter the cab because he couldn't climb the steps. And he had the

biggest smile on his face as he went up and down a few rows. He had no idea we set it on auto-steer to keep him on the straight and narrow.

- My husband and I work in his family's business. Our jobs require a lot of daily interaction with my in-laws. We also attend the same church on Sunday and I quickly learned there is an "assigned" family pew. Then my mother-in-law, who has spent hours preparing a wonderful Sunday family meal, expects us to join the family for food and afternoon games. I love my in-laws, but am I so wrong to wish for a few times when we can be "just us" with our friends?

All generations are needed on the farm.

The farm and the family need the best of all generations—wise mentors who have ridden the roller coaster of agriculture's economics and have a time-tested perspective of a changing world. We also need the energy, technology, understanding, and new ideas of younger generations. Together, we embrace diversity and challenges, experience and tradition. Let's respectfully include all generations in our goal to enjoy a joy-filled, lifelong journey on the farm. ❖

CHAPTER 5

"His problem may not be you!"

KNOWING YOUR ROLE AND RESPECTING YOUR VALUE

ometimes we women in agriculture are asked, "What are you? A farmer, a farm-her, a farm partner, a farm wife?" A good response might be, "I'm whatever I need to be to get the job done." And that's exactly what we Sisters in Agriculture do. We get the job done.

Along the way, we keep in mind that the struggle of negotiating with our spouses about what we do and how things are done is not a war; it's not "me versus the farm." We come together as a team on and off the farm. And when we feel pushed to the side, it's time to take a break with girlfriends, neighbors, or family members farther away.

Jolene's Experience

We Sisters in Agriculture work extremely hard and wear many hats. We get tired and perhaps weary, always wondering when enough is enough.

During my workshop titled *The Balancing Act: Ten Ideas to Relieve Stress and Bring Renewal to Our Farm and Family Life*, women repeatedly

share what they want. They feel they deserve to be respected for their roles and contributions to the family and the farm. And they're hungry for the men in their lives to express appreciation for the many hats they wear.

The lesson people glean from the workshop is this: You can ask for what you need. Perhaps your spouse will be eager in the giving but if he isn't, you can turn to your friends for support.

Insights from Our Sisters in Agriculture

- When my hubby said, "I could do it better by myself," I turned and walked toward the house. He never said that to me again.

- I just love it when my husband gives me "the look," meaning "I should know" or "that's a dumb question" or "don't you remember?" On one of the days I'd reached my limit with "the look," I marched up to my husband and said, "I'm doing the best I can with what I know. Until you start paying me, this is all you're going to get!"

- Here's my response for those tense moments when working with my spouse: "If you do not change your tone, I will find other ways to spend my time."

> You can ask for what you need.

- It was an insightful moment when I understood that land is just dirt and cows will become hamburger, but people and family, that's what really matters.

- When my husband starts yelling that I'm not doing it right, I walk away. We have the right to be treated with dignity and respect—and not be expected to know how to do everything.

- I describe myself as the "ghost writer" of the farm. I do the farming and a lot of the work – all "behind the scenes." For example, I do all the financial work in preparation for land rental agreements. Yet

when we sit at the kitchen tables, some of our older landowners only want my husband to do the talking. And when there's a question, my husband turns to me to share the answer. I call this "playing the game of perception." Does it need to change? Yes! Do we get the rental contract on our terms? Yes! Does my husband honor my work and "sneak in" the reality that I am the farmer? Yes! Remember: keep the bigger goal in mind as you chip away at stereotypes.

- An equipment salesman pulled into our driveway and parked near the farm house. I walked out of the kitchen to greet him as he asked, "Is the boss home?" I replied, "Yes I am. How might I help you?"

Cathy's Experience

I saw "deserved respect" modeled when my mom was called to assist my dad by pulling out a tractor he had gotten stuck in a field. Mom loaded us young kids into a pickup, drove to the field, and put us in the bed of the pickup for safe observation. Then she proceeded to climb onto the front tractor, the one that would do the pulling. Dad hooked the two with a big log chain, climbed onto the stuck tractor, and gave Mom the signal to go ahead. As her tractor crawled forward, the chain between the two tractors tightened. We watched and waited for Dad's tractor to move. Nothing.

Then the wheels on Mom's tractor began to spin. Dad yelled, "Stop! Can't you see I'm not moving?" She backed up the tractor and listened as Dad barked his instructions a second time. The scene repeated itself again, Dad yelling, Mom's tractor wheels spinning.

Then I watched as my mother calmly climbed down from the tractor and walked toward the pickup. Dad, still sitting on his tractor, yelled, "Where are you going? Can't you see the tractor is still stuck?"

My mother spun around and glared at my father. "I'm going home. Your yelling at me isn't helping. And I didn't get the tractor stuck in the first place. So the way I see it, you need me. Try getting the tractor out yourself." Needless to say, my dad's attitude changed in a hurry.

Maybe it's time we women on the farm reframe our thinking from "helping him" to "working on the farm." As one wife shared, "When my husband asks for help, I reply, 'Are you asking me to work with you?'" She said that this made a difference in how she is treated. As a result, she becomes a problem-solver and part of the project.

> Keep the bigger goal in mind.

Peak Season Challenges

Look out for personality changes during peak seasons such as planting, spraying, harvesting, calving, tax preparation, and so on. They may be related to lack of sleep, time constraints, financial pressures, expectations, regulations, weather, and more. Remember two things: this too will pass and it's not about you. So what can you do during these trying times?

- Appreciate the farm life you have. Where else do you get to work side by side with your husband?

- When there's mud on the floor, be grateful for the boots that brought him into the house.

- When you are tempted to be angry or resentful about the number of hours your husband spends in the barn, shop, or field, that's good news. You know where he is, and he could be in a lot worse places.

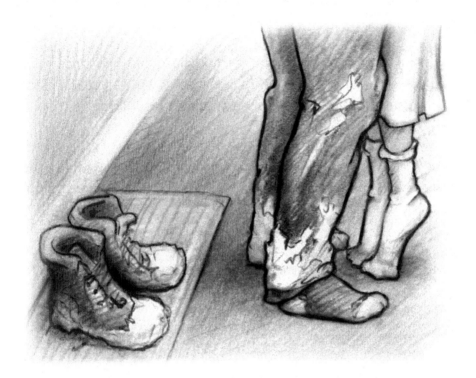

Keep in mind your spouse is not choosing the farm over you; he's choosing the farm for you and the family you're creating together.

Jolene's Experience

The phone rang. A young farm mom called wanting insight into positioning their family business for the next generation. When I asked about the family, she said their six children ranged from four months to 14 years. She also said her husband was a good yet busy farmer. This mom explained she was beginning to assume more of the farm responsibilities, including the bookwork, and hoped to "help out" even more. My response: "Your life must be crazy! Six wonderfully busy kids, a hard-working husband, a growing farm. And now you are accepting more farm responsibilities! Who's helping you?"

Insights from Our Sisters in Agriculture

- I was helping my mom sort through things when I opened the large bottom drawer of her dresser. It held some of the most beautiful gifts she'd been given over the years, all brand new, never used. A holiday tablecloth, a luxurious terry bathrobe, a box that held new pearl earrings, embroidered pillow cases, fluffy bath towels, Laura Ashley pajamas, and more. I looked at Mom and asked, "Mom, who are you saving these for—Dad's next wife?" Next time I was home, I noticed the new towels and special pajamas in the laundry. Way to go, Mom!

- It's OK to treat yourself to treats. It's OK and smart to ask for help. It's OK to do the work for your own health and fitness. It's OK to say "yes" and it's also OK to say "no."

Cathy's Experience

Early in our marriage, my husband and I committed to setting aside one night a week when, no matter what the season, we would have a date night. Looking back, perhaps there should have been additional rules.

Our date nights have consisted of shopping for groceries, stopping at the Dairy Queen after making a late-night parts run, and eating pizza from the local store. Some date nights included our two sons. But it never really mattered "what" we did; it was our commitment that counted.

Date nights don't have to be fancy.

Thirty-five years later, date nights still occur, and we probably look forward to them more now than we did early in our marriage. Commit to a date night. You'll never regret it!

Insights from Our Sisters in Agriculture

- I told my husband years ago: "You're stuck with me. Live with it!"

- Sometimes you need to pick up your husband's arms and put them around you if you need a hug.

- When you get a compliment . . . take it! And don't forget to give one!

- Take time to nurture friendships, especially with neighbors who may be experiencing the same trials as you. Remember to connect with friends and family, too. You will need several options as you walk through your years of agriculture.

- Friday night is our date night, farmer-style, me on the buddy seat of the tractor and my best buddy right next to me.

- Find a good friend willing and eager to listen and find time to do what you enjoy away from the farm with your friend.

- Silly me. I thought when we married, my husband would meet all of my needs. Most of those needs became expectations running around in my head of what he should say, how he should say it, and what he should do. When my expectations were not met, I became unhappy, grumpier, and more isolated. I finally realized what a terrible burden I was placing on him. A breakthrough in my happiness and our relationship happened when I realized it is my responsibility to keep things in perspective and prioritize what I need. I must then let my husband know what only he can fulfill. And sometimes we need to negotiate that. I've learned to seek and cultivate multiple resources to help-friends, family, church, neighbors, and organizations. As I gave to others and broadened my world, I received what I needed in return. This sure made me a lot more content and excited about my world on the farm. And it made my husband happy too, especially when I ask, "What do you need from me?"

Who is helping you?

Jolene's Experience

During a family business consultation, I noted how weary the mother looked. A 50% owner of a progressive, labor-intensive business, she held most of the employee management responsibilities and worked long hours by their sides. She did her job exceptionally well.

At the end of our conversation she said, "I'm off to a school board meeting. There's a movement underway to elect me as the next president. I'm trying to decide if I should serve a third term." Having just reviewed her family/business roles and responsibilities, I commented, "Wow! You already have a full plate. Is serving as president of the school board adding another major job?" Then she replied, "You know, if I wasn't on the school board, I would never get off of this farm. I need this to gain perspective for my mind and my heart."

Insights from Our Sisters in Agriculture

- Nurture friendships, especially women friends. You need them.

- If you are struggling, talk now before you quit talking. Build a team. Ask for help.

- My husband is a member of a commodity marketing club that meets regularly. I call it his "support group." I decided I needed a group, too. I'm a city girl and brand new member of Women Living on the Farm. I often wonder, "Is this crazy or am I? Do you have any short-cuts? How on earth do you do that?" So I called a neighbor I had yet to meet and said, "I need your help." She called a few other women in our neighborhood and we set up a gathering once a month in each other's homes. No worries about serving food or cleaning. Mostly we laugh together, and I learn a lot! I'm not sure I would have survived my first year of being married to a farmer without these neighbors.

> Neighbors are "sisters" next door.

Never forget, as women on the farm, you have great value, some of which you've never imagined. Why, even your weight can be an asset. As one woman shared, "Have you ever been asked to be the counter balance for moving a long elevator or grain tube?" See, he does need you! ❖

CHAPTER 6

"Sometimes you just have to say no."

JUGGLING LIFE WITH A SMILE

A favorite speaking peer is Kathy Peterson of PeopleWorks Inc. She craftily demonstrates the multitude of roles we Sisters in Agriculture assume. After bringing on stage a willing volunteer, she has the audience call out a role or responsibility—wife, mom, volunteer, teacher, gardener, tractor driver, chauffeur, livestock caretaker, bookkeeper, and more. With each addition, she tosses a blown-up balloon to the volunteer, asking her to keep all balloons in the air at the same time. With a few, it's easy, but it doesn't take long until the balloons start to drop, and everyone bursts out laughing.

What is the lesson? That it's not always the amount of work we do or the number of roles we play that creates the overload. Instead, it's not allowing any balls to drop without feeling guilty. What would allow you to put down a few of those balloons so you might juggle the rest with a smile on your face?

Jolene's Experience

At my presentations, I often hear about informal and formal gatherings of women who have a need for togetherness, laughter, learning, support, and caring. Some of the group names include:

- **The Sag Hags**—women who live on Sagert Drive

- **Whine or Wine Club**—women who drink only two glasses each at a gathering

- **Stitch and Gritch**—this group routinely meets in the basement of the church for quilting projects and more.

We are
stronger
together.

In the 1980s, those in Midwest agriculture were going through a particularly tenuous time of high stress. We were dealing with dire net worth loss, foreclosures, bankruptcies, depression, and suicides. All of us needed hope and help, so thirteen women with a connection to agriculture reached out to one another. We knew we must "march to a different drum" or we, too, could be drowned by the negative. We met routinely for more than a decade and to this day, many of us keep in touch.

If you look at your world closely, you'll see everyday people doing exceptional things. Then when you meet, you might consider following this agenda we used at our life-saving gatherings: 1) State something good that has happened since the last time we met; 2) Talk about a realistic concern or problem you're working on and need help with 3) Share a dream, goal, vision for the future.

Only one thing I know for sure: we women in agriculture need each other for the tough times, for the everyday times, and for the celebration times.

Cathy's Experience

On my bucket list was running a 5K race so I hired a great trainer, Jill, and within six weeks I did it! Next up was running a 13.1K half-marathon race. As Jill and I were on a conditioning run with six of 10 miles completed, I suddenly felt extremely fatigued and nauseated. After resting a bit, I tried to go on but could barely walk. Then insightful Jill stated, "I think we're done running for today. In fact, we're done until you see a doctor."

The medical doctor was clear. "Cathy, your body is trying to tell you something. The stress of your job, the running, your responsibilities add up. Perhaps you should listen to your body."

We women in agriculture get so used to the pressures of our work, home, farm, and family needs and responsibilities, I realized my inability to say "no" was slowly killing me. I needed to change. Most of all I learned that sometimes you just need to shorten the list of things that "must be done" for others and put things on that list that help take care of you.

———

Remember, it's okay to vent, but it's more important to acknowledge what you can and can't change, decide on an alternative reaction, and move in a positive way. And be careful who you invite to your pity party. They need to know that a "dump load" of facts or feelings is not you over the long haul. But still, you need them to be present, listen, care—and help you move on. Keeping perspective on the farm is a challenge as our world of farming and ranching is a consuming force. We live where we work and we work where we live. We identify our home, our work, and who we are with terms relating to "the farm." That's great, until we choose to or are forced to leave the farm. Then what? I believe all farmers should ask themselves, "If I could not farm, what would I do?" I believe the answer to that question is beneficial to Plan A (what you are currently doing) and is a powerful pre-emptive support system if you need to consider Plan B (a different option).

If I could not farm, what would I do?

As a professional speaker, I meet thousands of people in agriculture each year. As a writer for several websites and magazines, many more contact me. They'd like time to share a conversation, a story, a concern with me or even ask a question. So, I listen to their words, their emotions, the silence of their depression, their shouts of anger and unfairness. I witness people in transition. What they've taught me is that having a Plan B is helpful even if you never plan to leave the farm. Looking at a mental option of what else you could (or would) do adds strength for creativity, necessary risk taking, and flexibility in today's changing times. It's also the next step for those who retire or must change plans due to health or financial problems. Plan B reduces the paralyzing, underlying fear of thinking, "I must succeed because this is the only thing I can do."

We in agriculture have many talents and skills. Farming and ranching require them of us. From scientist and mechanic to public relations and marketing, from food and fiber specialist to doctor and decision maker, from employee and financial manager to lobbyist and leader, never underestimate your competencies. Run with your vision and passion and put them to full use on your farm. And, if you choose to start over or change direction, remember, we live in a country where history has proven that opportunities abound.

There is great wisdom in this quote by Alexander Graham Bell: "When one door closes, another opens but we often look so long and so regretfully upon the closed door that we do not see the one which has opened for us."

It's when we build on our strengths, overcome our weaknesses, tolerate our limitations, and keep things in perspective that we can build a strong foundation for ourselves and our working team.

Insights from Our Sisters in Agriculture

- Don't forget the mini-celebrations. If your farmer offers to take you out to eat, drop everything and go!

Don't forget mini- celebrations!

- I was petrified of life without my "label." I was a farmer but due to finances, we lost the farm. Do you know what happened? I shared my story and my talents. Life outside of farming embraced me.

- My husband is a perfectionist. About the time I drive him nuts with my shortcuts, I remind him, "Gosh, I can't be all that bad because you are a perfectionist and you chose me!" It's good to remember, you don't have to give up and let go of everything just because you

married a farmer. You were chosen "as is."

- My husband loves homemade blackberry jam and insists I make it for him every year. When the blackberries are ripe, I announce I'll be making jam on a certain day and he will need to find something to do. "It's a sticky mess and you shouldn't bother me," I tell him. When he leaves, I get out my jam jars and the cases of Smucker's Blackberry jam that I have purchased. Then I heat it up, put it into my sterilized jars, and seal them. Never in the last 50 years has he known that I don't make his "homemade" blackberry jam!

- When you think you can't do anymore, know that THIS TOO SHALL PASS. ❖

CHAPTER 7

"For better, for worse,

the critters come first!"

PRIORITIES ON THE FARM

Animals are creatures of habit. On our farms and ranches, they require consistent nutrition, temperature, and attention. Caring for their welfare often creates a challenge for scheduling farm and family activities. How often have we heard, "Once the chores are done we can _____" or "We'll need to find someone to do the chores so we can leave."

Meeting the needs of our animals often trumps everything else. But it's also a part of farm life that brings many joys and teaches valuable life lessons. Few things beat watching a newborn animal take its first steps or the pride that grows from building a herd. Most of all, caring for animals can help "grow" our children. By consistently doing daily chores, they see the progress and positive results

> Caring for animals "grows" our children.

of accepting responsibility. They turn away from the concept of "entertain me" to adopting an attitude of "I'll care for you." In this way, they build their confidence and compassion because they have a direct influence.

You'll see how the language of animal agriculture finds its way into everyday happenings. Don't be offended if, while you are pregnant, you're asked when you will calve or when the next pregnancy check is scheduled. Or if you're cleaning the house, you may be asked if you're nesting like the sows do before birth.

Similarly, here's what your children might hear: "The farrowing house is cleaner than your room" and "Finish your meal. The cattle eat better than you do." They learn the cycle of life has sad times and happy times and, as animal caretakers, they become a responsible party in the journey.

Cathy's Experience

With the due date of our first child getting close, I was uncomfortable. One evening, my husband and I had been in bed for about an hour when I began tossing and turning, covers off, then on, then off again. I couldn't

get comfortable and my husband quietly whispered to me, "Cathy, you're rooting around in here like a sow getting ready to farrow." Three hours later, my water broke and as I woke my sleeping husband to tell him, he exclaimed, "I told you! Just like an old sow!"

Insights from Our Sisters in Agriculture

- At our house, the animals are fed first. Then we eat.

- Mom always said, "Don't learn to milk cows." I never listened to her. Dumb me.

- I grew up on a vegetable farm but married a cow/calf man. Shortly after our wedding, my father-in-law and I were heading down the county blacktop. I oooooed and ahhhhed as we passed a beautiful animal in the nearby pasture. "Look at that beautiful heifer!" Wrong! It was a big bull, not a female who had not yet calved. Ten years later, I'm still hearing about it!

> *Animal agriculture comes with its own language.*

- A pig trailer saved our marriage. Before that, my husband thought we should just "walk" the pregnant sows up to the farrowing house. This inevitably turned into a "chasing good time" as the pregnant sows took off in the opposite direction. So finally, he bought a pig mover. We load the sows into it, drive to the farrowing house, and let them out. Happy farmer, happy sows, happy me.

- Helping my husband clean the steer lots, I was appointed the job of opening and closing the gates with the help of my grandson. My husband, in a rush to get things done, wanted me to hurry up and open the gates. "I don't have all day!" he yelled. I told him I was going as fast as I could. Then my grandson piped up, "Grandpa, don't yell at her. She's all you got!"

- "Honey, all you have to do is hold the gate." That really means it's your responsibility and your fault for what ultimately happens during

livestock sorting time. Instead, offer to be the one who brings the animals to the gate area. Let him "man" the gate!

- We show pigs at fairs. I participate to give my husband support as best I can. But I refuse to learn how to hook up the livestock trailer to the pickup. I know if I learned, I'd receive a call or text from my hubby saying, "You go ahead and load up the pigs and get them to the show. I'll meet you there." Not going to happen!

- Husbands don't always transfer what they know from the farm to personal life. My husband can milk cows and be covered in cow manure, but baby poop and breast milk creep him out.

- Being married to a hog farmer means I have vaccinated hogs on the Fourth of July, baled hay during the parade I didn't see, called the police to notify my husband at softball practice that the hogs were out, and chased hogs well after my due date. The variety and excitement make for an interesting life.

- I wasn't in favor of building a hog finishing facility because I thought we had enough work with the livestock we already had. I was assured by my husband and son that the two of them would be able to handle it. I would not have to be involved at all. They lied! On a market day as we were loading a truck with hogs, one turned and charged to the other end of the pen. I was in the way and ended up facing south on a northbound hog. When I finally fell off the hog, the men cheered and said, "Hey, you almost made it eight seconds. Think we should enter you in the rodeo contest?"

> *Celebrate when and wherever you can.*

- My friend is a city-raised gal. One day we were driving down the road and a bull and cow were "going at it." (Well, you get the picture.) In shock, she turned to me and asked, "Do they really do that right out in the open?" I quietly replied, "No, usually they have a dark stall with music and candles."

- I give my favorite cows names. For example: Freckles (she's so cute), Miss Moose (she's so big), Mona Moose (Miss Moose's daughter), and One Hung Low (because she had mastitis and was being treated for an inflamed udder). My husband carries a book and writes down their ear tag numbers. How boring.

Cathy's Experience

Years ago, my husband and I had just purchased our first hog facility, which meant we had no extra money for hired labor. We were the only ones in this together. As someone who grew up showing show cattle, I didn't know a thing about raising hogs, but I was more than willing to learn. Looking back 30+ years, I think my husband must have been desperate for any kind of help in the barn. Anyone who raises livestock (particularly hogs) knows that one's patience is tested, voices get louder, and facial expressions (insert eye rolling here) replace talking. (You get the idea.)

One day while we were moving sows from one room to another, it didn't go so well. I was in the way (most of the time) while my husband thought I could read his mind. After chasing the sows up and down the hallway numerous times, he announced, "I can do this faster without you." I was livid. I gave him "the look," spun around in my fashionable knee high Tingley boots, and stomped off to another area of the barn slamming every door I could along the way.

"I'm right.
And so
are you."

Two hours later and still mad, I headed to an area of the barn to change my clothes. I could see he had already changed clothes, so I quickly changed and walked out of the barn to the house. As I closed the door to the hog barn, my husband stood waiting for me. He stared at me and said, "I told you working with sows isn't easy, and you can't take things personally if we're going to make this work."

He was right. I knew it, and so did he. He then put his arm around my waist and we headed to the house for lunch. Whatever disagreement we had in the barn earlier that morning stayed there. But when we returned after lunch, our arguments promptly picked up where we left off.

Throughout our years working together in those barns, we've encountered many days like that. However, I can proudly say we have mastered the art of "what goes on in the barn absolutely stays in the barn."

Insights from Our Sisters in Agriculture

- When I complain about the smell on the farm, my husband replies, "That's the smell of money, honey."

- When you open your refrigerator, you will probably find vials of vaccines and medicine beside your ketchup and salad dressing.

- One of the most feared proclamations: "Come on, the cows are out!!!"

- The dreaded pitch-dark nighttime phone call: "I believe your black Angus cows are on the road."

- As a young girl, I raced outside after receiving the mandate "Help now! The pigs are out!" That's when I discovered my dad had a whole new language. I also learned that I was not to repeat that language or I'd be in trouble.

> There are funnies everywhere on the farm. Let the laughter out!

- Be sure to learn the proper name for an animal. A heifer may be a Hereford, but not all Herefords are heifers.

- Never pet the bull by mistake!

- If you're trying to tempt the horses to do what you want using feed as the bait, make sure you have a head start on them.

- Always put on your seat belt if you're driving or riding in a pick-up. You may be chasing cattle in an open field only to experience prairie dog holes, speed bumps, indented cattle trails, sharp turns, sudden stops, and fast accelerations.

- The smaller your wrist, the more you may be called upon to unplug an auger, help a sow birth pigs, or artificially inseminate a heifer.

- As I was preparing supper one evening, my husband came into the kitchen and asked if he could use my food processor to grind dewormer pellets for our pigs. I just looked at him and kept on cooking.

- Our ram is named Rambo for a reason. Watch your backside or you'll find yourself flat on your back.
- During the sex education curriculum of health class, my kids were the first to offer the examples. As the teacher was explaining "twins," our son interrupted, "That's nothing. You could be a sow birthing fourteen pigs!" Most farm kids know more about "the birds and the bees" than they do about birds or bees.

Care for the animals on a farm is a 24-hour-a-day 365-days-a-year job regardless of weather or our own personal needs. As my friend shared, "I've told our kids, those animals depend on us. They need feed and water, a clean and comfortable place to live, and our care and attention." And through that understanding, those animals of the farm have taught us life lessons of great value. ✣

CHAPTER 8

"This darn equipment!"

BREAKDOWNS, PARTS RUNS, AND A SENSE OF HUMOR

"If he's not handy, you darn well better be." These emphatic words were shared by a Sister in Agriculture as she exclaimed, "You can't begin to imagine the number of moving parts on the farm! And oh yes, the equipment breaks down." What we've learned is without an engineering degree, lots of experience, practical wisdom, adaptability, creativity, patience, and lots of money, the mechanics and machines on the farm will truly test every relationship.

Don't forget to say thanks.

If you are sent on the mission of "going after equipment and farm parts," you'll find the experience easier if you are prepared—and you take along a sense of humor. You can even be the bright spot in the day for the person greeting you behind the equipment parts counter.

Always remember, those who work in the parts department are key to the productivity of your business. Bring them treats, especially at the busy times like planting and harvest. They'll certainly remember you. On rainy days, a long line of people will need their expertise so especially on those days, bring your patience and appreciation.

And while you're spending long hours running that equipment, it's a real health benefit to keep stretch therapy bands in each tractor, truck, and combine. (They're often used by physical therapy patients.) At peak planting and harvest times or in long hauling lines, you may be sitting in that machine for hours, day after day. But if it's on auto-steer or you stop for a minute, pull out the band and stretch your body parts. As one woman shared at a conference, "I watched my daughter-in-law in the grain cart pull out her band. The next thing I knew, my son who was running the combine responded by pulling out his band. They were stretching limbs, moving blood, and laughing. It makes for healthier, happier times."

Of utmost importance is keeping your own tool box well supplied and handy. Don't leave home without duct tape, baling wire, boots, gloves, clean rags, dental floss, granola bars, paper towels, wet wipes. And oh yes! The tools: hammer, multipurpose tool, crescent wrench, flashlight, a pair of coveralls, and your sense of humor.

Insights from Our Sisters in Agriculture

- If you are the one expected to put a machine together, you'd better be the one to have taken it apart! Often we didn't take them apart, but we end up going after the parts.

- Do not put his tools away where they belong; he only remembers where he left them.

- I asked my husband why the farm continues to have his father drive machinery, especially since he's had two minor accidents. My husband's response: "It's not his fault he can't see well." Some things are not accidents, they are stupidity.

- When doing a parts run, come back with the parts and a candy bar for your husband. A chocolate treat goes a long way to brighten someone's day. And while you're at it, bring back two candy bars— one for you, too!

- Weighing our grain wagons in the barn's narrow alleyway means getting the big tractor's dual tires close to the barn's old stone foundation so the wagon can be centered on the scale. I have at max only a three-inch space on the foundation side. When I drive too close, black rubber marks appear on the walls and the tires show the scuffing. It made my husband quite unhappy. My solution? I painted white reflective stripes for the tractor's front tires to follow. I also learned that, if I goof up, black shoe polish works well to darken the side of the tire.

Be creative with your farm repairs.

- My husband asked, "Can you run to town and pick up a part?" Off I went. But he didn't say I needed the pickup to transport this large part. It barely fit into our Tahoe SUV.

- Hand tools around the farm can have very specific uses, names, and numbers. My husband was underneath the belly of the combine shouting to me, "Go get me the wrench." In the tool box I saw multiple wrenches: open end, box end, crescent, Allen, ratchet/socket. So I grabbed five options. After handing them to him, he said, "I didn't mean that one." Jeepers.

When it comes to an equipment breakdown, you'll hear numerous times, "I used to be able to take it apart and fix it by myself. Now I have to wait for a technician to run a diagnostic review. He'll tell me I need to replace an entire component. Then I'll wait several days for the expensive parts to appear . . . and then wait for the technician to return for the installation. Whatever happened to a fix with duct tape and baling wire?"

Your children and grandchildren will love riding along when you go to town, even when you have to run for parts. It's a treat for those who work in our implement dealerships to see little ones, too. A Sister in Agriculture explained that was the setting for an insightful conversation with Grandpa, Dad, and Little Grandson Tommy. They were no stranger to Don, the salesman at the John Deere dealership. But Don quickly noticed that the usual chatty Tommy was quiet and wearing a frown. Don asked, "Tommy, what are you thinking about?" Tommy replied, "My mom doesn't think my dad gets paid enough." Grandpa and Dad didn't say a word, but I imagine there's a conversation needing to take place.

Some of the very best times with our children are when they are safely buckled into the tractor's "buddy seat" and we head to the fields one on

one. We're surrounded by nature while doing the important work on the farm. It's prime time to listen, ask, respond, care, and converse. It's also time to be quiet and let the acres of the farm pass by.

The bond that forms among family members as they work together on the land is the start of the legacy of that land—a love of the farm that passes from generation to generation.

Jolene's Advice

When you are sent to find and pick up equipment parts, complete this checklist:

1.) Take a picture on your phone or camera of the part and the piece of equipment from which it came.

2.) Write down the make and model of the equipment.

3.) Write down the parts numbers for what you need.

4.) Take the broken part with you.

> Take the broken part with you.

5.) Don't assume that because your husband "called ahead" that people in the parts department won't have questions for you.

6.) Be sure the part you are sent for will fit into the vehicle you will be driving.

7.) As you leave, turn on your husband's cell phone. Give him specific instructions that he can't turn it off and must answer if it rings.

8.) Look carefully over the parts list before you leave the farm in case he has written something on the list that was meant for personal eyes only.

9.) Before the parts man records your purchase on his invoice, I always ask, "When he puts in this part, is he going to need something else he's not thought about? O-ring, seal, cotter pin?" Then I call my

hubby or I bring home more. Sometimes I tell the parts man, "Put anything in that box you think he might need. If he doesn't need it, may I return it within three days?" I've saved myself many a mile with that question. And I often hear my mechanic husband say, "I should replace that as well while I have the equipment torn apart."

10.) While at the parts counter, be ready to answer those surprise questions such as "Do you know the serial number?" or "Do you know who drove it last?" Here are my favorite questions: "Is the tractor facing east or west?" and "Which end of the hydraulic hose do you need, the male or the female end?" To the second question I replied, "At your age, if you don't know, I'm not going to tell you!"

Note: Include this *Going After Parts Checklist* with your marriage certificate.

Cathy's Experience

Oh, I so remember the angst I felt the day my oldest son was scheduled for his pre-school screening. I was your typical mother, both concerned and excited as I watched him take the hand of the screener and walk to the table across the room. I observed anxiously as he pointed to objects and confidently performed the various tasks asked of him. Once the screening was finished, the screener returned my four year old to me and asked to have a word with me. The screener told me my son had done very well in all the basic areas except for one: identifying his colors. "Mrs. Riley, you have a bright little boy, but he needs work with identifying his colors, and he'll need to be retested."

What? He knows his colors. Perhaps he was just nervous. So I asked, "What do you mean?"

The screener replied, "Well, when I pointed to the red crayon, he responded 'That's International.' Then I pointed to the blue crayon, and your son responded with 'That's Ford.'" I began to smile. The screener then said, "And when I pointed to the green crayon, he replied with 'That one is easy; it's John Deere.'"

It turns out my little farmer knew his "basic" machinery colors. So I smiled at her and said, "Let me explain." Then I asked if she knew the color of an International tractor and she said, "Yes, it's red." A Ford tractor? She responded, "Blue." I smiled, and she did too. Then she laughed, "And a John Deere is green."

> Farm equipment is identified by colors.

Needless to say, our son passed his pre-school screening with flying (farming) colors! Some of us grew up playing with tractors. The lucky ones still do.

Farmers wait with bated breath for the announcement of dates for farm shows showcasing industry updates and displaying the latest and greatest equipment. Be sure you attend as well! You'll discover your farmer is like a kid in a candy store, discovering temptations aisle after aisle. You'll hear things he rarely shares—his dreams and goals, his likes and dislikes, his awe of the industry. Also expect to wait around awhile as he asks company representatives questions he's held in his head for a long time.

This critical side of your farmer deserves your respect, time, and patience. And as one of our Sisters in Agriculture shared, "While at the farm show, be sure to leave the checkbook and credit cards at home!" ❖

CHAPTER 9

"The more I deal with people,
the more I like pigs."

COMMUNICATION CHALLENGES

Mind reading is not an acceptable form of communication. Neither is yelling, cussing, ignoring, rolling eyes, slamming doors, walking away, or making obscure hand gestures, grunts, heavy sighs, mumbles. Just think what would happen if you exhibited those behaviors in any other kind of working relationship! Doesn't your family deserve your best?

In agriculture, giving instructions comes in common styles. A few are:
"Watch and then you'll know."
"Get out of my way. I can do it quicker."
"Read my mind!"

It would be so much better if we could learn from a teacher and repeat the process to become efficient, then ask questions for clarification along the way. Instead, most of us learn by doing, making mistakes, and turning to others for a better option.

> Mind reading
> is not
> enough.

Jolene's Experience

Since it was a cold harvest morning, my husband started the pickup so the engine could warm while he took the first wagon out to the corn field. Shortly after, I hopped into that warm vehicle to drive out to the field and

pick him up. As I started to back the truck away from the barn, it began to accelerate on its own. The more I pressed on the brake, the faster it went. It stopped only when I crashed into the grain bin, denting the bottom panel and shearing off bolts. I sat shaking and wondering, "What the heck happened?" It's then I noticed that to make the pickup idle faster and warm up quicker, he had wedged a small rectangular block underneath the brake to hold down the accelerator. The result? The more I pressed on the brake, the more I was stomping on the accelerator.

There are days when divorce is just not good enough.

Insights from Our Sisters in Agriculture

- The toughest form of communication is no communication.

Communication is a verb.

- There are times it's best to say nothing and other times when it's best to just walk away. You can always talk to the dog.

- I've said to my farmer, "You're going to need some patience because I've got some questions."

- If you want something, you have to ask for it. Husbands never get your hints.

- When you see your husband fixing the corn head on a beautiful, sunny October day, do not ask how things are going. In fact, try to avoid him at all costs.

- Be sure you know what document you are signing. Ask questions. You may even want to get an independent legal explanation. As one wife shared, "Even though I'm not involved in the farming operation, signing a personal loan guarantee for a farm loan has consequences."

- We'd had a bunch of rain so my husband thought it was a good time to tow our problem tractor into town to the repair shop. I was the puller (in the old farm pickup); he was the pullee (in the broken-down tractor). Because this is not my favorite job, I specifically asked my husband, "What do you want me to do?" He said, "Just put on your flashers, keep the chain taut, don't go too fast and turn right at the bowling alley." So I did. But oh my, the turn at the bowling alley took us down a really muddy side alley. We were spinning wheels, slipping and sliding all over the place, and we barely reached the end. Finally, I made the last turn into the repair shop. As I got out of the pickup, my hubby greeted me with his arms crossed. Fuming, he shouted, "Why on earth did you go down that mud alley!?" I told him, "I did as you said, 'Turn right at the bowling alley.'" He replied, "Well, you know I didn't mean the bowling alley; you know I meant turn right at the gas station."

> "I will help, but if you yell, I will quit!"

- I had to make sure my husband understood some of my rules of communication that related to "helping" him. My main rule? "I will help. But if you yell, I will quit!' And of course the first time we were sorting hogs, he didn't like the way I was "manning the gate." Next came his yelling commands and four-letter words. So I just closed the gate and walked to the house. He now understands my main rule.

- Too many times I've been expected to know what time I should be in the field, where to park the grain cart, or when a delivery of feed was due to arrive. I give up. I've told my husband I haven't had time to take Mind Reading: 101. Would he remind me to sign up the next time the class is offered?

- Why is it when he's giving me instructions or telling me something important he does so as he's walking out the door or heading down the steps? Sometimes I find myself trotting after him so I can stop him, turn him around, and ask him to repeat himself. If he wants me to really understand him, I need to read his lips. Maybe then I have a chance to understand his mind.

———

Jolene's Experience

Harvest is not always easy, especially when Mother Nature brings lots of rain and mud. With a weather forecast of heavy snow, we were determined to finish our last field. At two in the morning, I'd just picked up a full combine hopper of grain into my grain wagon. Over the radio system my husband instructed, "Go ahead and take this load to the gateway. I'll bring the rest on the combine."

Patience, please!

So I turned my tractor and wagon toward the fence row. I was at the second hill when my tractor's wheels started spinning out on muddy, slippery ground. I knew I had to stop before they dug in deeper. When my husband turned the combine at the end of his pass, he noticed my tractor lights were still in the contour of the field. He radioed, "I said, go ahead and take that to the gate. I'll bring the rest."

I replied, "No. I'll wait right here."
"No, take that load to gate."
"No, I'll wait right here.
"Are you stuck?"
"Yes, I'll wait right here."
Click. Silence.

When it comes to communicating with a quiet, silent, or "too busy for you" partner, Robert M. Bramson, PhD, suggests in his book *Coping With Difficult People* (Random House, 2012) that we ask an open-ended question and give the silent or unresponsive person a friendly but silent stare. Then we wait.

However, when it comes to a spouse, you can ask the open-ended question, wait a few minutes, and then add, "Gosh, I assume by your silence you agree with me." That usually brings an immediate answer. If one is not forthcoming, then do what you want to do. He had his chance to provide input.

Silence
means
consensus.

Jolene's Experience

For a time, we were a sales representative for a seed company. We knew that during the rush of planting time—especially one dictated by less-than-favorable weather—operations were 24/7. So one night at midnight, my husband was planting our fields and I was "manning" the seed warehouse. The phone rang and a customer said, "I know it's late, but I bet you heard the forecast, too. I just need three more bags to get this field finished."

"No problem. We've got that number in the warehouse. Would you like it delivered to your farmstead or to a field?"

"Gosh, if you could bring it to the field, that would be great. Here are the directions. Cross the river bridge, turn left the second chance you get. Go a couple of miles or so to the jog in the road and turn left. Keep going a ways, and then turn right at that old house that burnt down a few years ago."

I just couldn't keep the laughter in. I replied, "OK, but it's pretty dark out. Is there still a big pile of ashes where the house burnt so I know where to turn?"

Insights from Our Sisters in Agriculture

- My husband does not communicate well. His idea of solving a problem is not talking for two or three days. It's so frustrating.

- I don't know whether my husband thinks I don't care about what he's doing, that I don't need to know, or that he doesn't want to waste his or my time talking about farm things to me. The bottom line is I do care. I may need to know, and I'm worth the investment of a few minutes of communication time.

- How often I have heard, "I can't get this! ##**!## to work!" to which I've replied, "It helps to read the manual."

- If I had a manual for hand signals, the first one I would look up is "What the heck does it mean if his hand is spinning in the air?" And no, the equipment is not hooked up to the Power Takeoff (PTO) shaft!

- Wouldn't it be great to have a manual titled *Hand Signals Used on Farms and Ranches*? Then I would add photos and graphics so I can easily understand all of his directions.

- My brother-in-law from Florida wanted to try farming in the Midwest, so one fall my husband "taught" him to run the grain cart. The first day, he forgot to shut off the cart's auger while my husband was unloading the combine's grain into his cart. The result? Very rapid corn transfer from the combine to the cart and immediately to the ground. That day, my brother-in-law learned a whole new set of hand signals—and an ear-full of expectations.

- I just wish my husband could hear himself. As I'm driving the tractor, slowly creeping back to hook on to the hayrack, he would shout, "Go ahead. Come back." I put my foot on the brake and got the giggles. What should I do? Go ahead or back up?

- As I walked through the barnyard, I saw my husband standing near a large steel gate. He asked, "Honey, would you just grab a hold of that end? We're going to move it." Of course, he assumes I can lift it, that I know where he's going with it and where to place it. I've learned to stop before I grab on and ask him to explain the details. It sure saves a lot of time, pulled muscles, and frustration when we talk first, then lift.

- My husband asked me to work the ground prior to planting. Because this was my first time driving our big tractor, he gave these few instructions: "Rabbit is fast; turtle is slow. This raises, this lowers." Then he left. By the end of the day, I had finally figured it out. In fact, I was proud of the good job I'd completed. When I returned to the farmstead, I asked how I did. He replied with a question: "What happened to the driveway behind the grove?" Oops, I had plowed it up.

  Rabbit is fast; turtle is slow.

- My husband gave directions by "road kill." He'd say, "Remember where our neighbor hit that big buck? Turn there." He'd also say, "Remember where that pheasant flew out of the grass along the side of the road and hit our windshield? That's the field where you need to bring the wagon."

- Be gracious when accepting feedback from your spouse. More than once I've had to bite my tongue after power washing a hog barn. I've asked my husband "how did I do" only to be met with his response "it depends whether or not you're done washing." I've learned to accept I will never, ever wash a barn room that's clean enough for him. My husband has also accepted that any time I'm willing to wash a barn, that's one barn he doesn't have to wash himself. We both win.

One thing we've learned, most men and women on the farm think and communicate differently than each other because of their completely different perspectives.

For example, I look out the kitchen window and see the swing hanging from the shade of our big old maple tree. I think of grandchildren laughing with glee as they soar to the sky. My husband looks out the same window and sees fields of corn growing. He thinks of weeds and insects, and he wonders if it's going to rain. I am geared to "people and pictures"; he is geared to "production and details." I talk aloud to solve a problem; he quietly thinks and then acts, often without talking.

Different isn't wrong.

This doesn't mean one style is right and one is wrong. It's just different. It also creates challenges in communication. ❖

CHAPTER 10

"For richer, for poorer."

MONEY DOES MATTER

Be wise with money because money does matter. It influences or drives the business, personal goals, and relationships. When it comes to financial knowledge of the farm, women have different levels of knowledge and involvement. Which of these describes your role?

1.) Some women serve as the CFO and bookkeeper, entering all financial data and reporting information. In this role, you pay the bills; record all transactions; and create documents such as the cash flow, net worth statement, key ratios for benchmark analysis and tax information. You meet with advisors and provide information that's crucial to decision making and the viability of the operation. Your financial leadership is needed and respected. You may or may not be financially compensated for your work.

> *Whatever your role, always ask questions.*

2.) Some women aren't in charge of finances but receive financial information. They have access to documents and can discuss reports. In this role, your input is included regarding major purchases and management of debt.

3.) Some women are "in the dark," knowing little of the overall financial picture of the farm business. They are not included in discussions or meetings with advisors. In this role, you have no idea about farm income or where the money comes from or where it goes.

Whatever your role, always ask questions. Regardless of your involvement, understand that most farm business loans require a spouse's signature as a personal loan guarantee, even if you're not an owner or included in financial decisions. Know what you are signing including the use and terms of the loan. Be aware of the consequences of your signature or lack of it. As one of our Sisters in Agriculture shared, "I know I'm signing a loan even though I have no control about what happens in the business. But if I don't sign, the farm won't get its operating loan. It's a between-a-rock-and-a-hard-place situation."

Also, take a class and attend farm events and seminars. Learn more about grain marketing, accounting, production practices, and future trends. A better understanding of your business can make your partnership stronger. After all, two heads are always better than one.

Cathy's Experience

In our household, my husband has always done the books. His attention to detail and natural ability to understand numbers and financial ratios—coupled with my 40-hour off-the-farm job—made him the logical choice to be the keeper of our farm's books. I often wish I could transfer all the knowledge he has in his head to mine. Come to find out, so does he.

> I often wish I could transfer all the knowledge he has in his head to mine.

It wasn't until a recent tax appointment I realized how much I didn't know about our family's farming operation. The two of us had sat through a two-hour appointment with our accountant and tax preparer. My husband answered the majority of the questions and provided documentation so the taxes for our two entities could be filed. And while I was able to answer a question or two fairly intelligently, I had to admit I knew next to nothing financially about our operations. Did our tax preparer notice how little I knew? I vowed to find a way to become more involved.

Money matters.

On our way home that day, my husband pointed out that I needed to take more interest in the financial aspects of our operation. He didn't enjoy seeing my "deer in the headlights" look in that meeting. We agreed I'd become more involved in the financial end. However, we had two major obstacles to overcome. I had to be willing to "follow his process"; he had to stop assuming any question I asked would be taken as my "questioning" his process.

Today, my spouse is still the master bookkeeper and I continue to learn "his process." Thank goodness we're making progress.

In the best of family business scenarios, conversations about farm finances is not a taboo issue. That doesn't mean the discussion about money is easy, especially during roller-coaster times of agricultural prices and income or a balance sheet of increasing short- and long-term debt.

The common expression of "asset rich, cash poor" tells the financial story of most farm businesses. Very few farms operate debt free and with cash on hand. Instead, they use operating loans to meet the annual and seasonal needs of the business. Yet, they have "investments" to manage such as machinery and livestock. And most farms have a land base that comes with its own financial terms for ownership, rental contracts, and leases. The challenge is, if you sell the investments for cash, you have nothing to create cash.

Get involved and informed.

Striking the balance of debt and assets, farm and personal income, and wants and needs is always a test of finances.

If you are an owner by titled property or live in a state that recognizes common law marriage and you meet those requirements—or if the income and debt of the farm affects your personal living and lifestyle—then get involved and informed.

If the farm operation has legal or other protocol that excludes you from attending financial meetings, it's important that your spouse represent your best interests in closed financial discussions and actions. This means he listens to you and your questions before the meetings and gives you information that directly affects your interests.

Keeping a spouse "in the dark" can set up a scary scenario.

Insights from Our Sisters in Agriculture

- When I married my farmer, I had no idea that purchasing land, equipment, animals, machinery, facilities, and supplies meant making a huge financial commitment. I had no idea that the loans or payments would include so many digits before the decimal point. When my friends in town complain about their house mortgage, I just listen. There's no comparison.

- I'm to do as I'm told. My husband and his bookkeeper handle all of the finances of the farm. He puts a loan paper in front of me and demands, "Sign it." He also has his own personal checking account and only puts a minimum amount into a joint account so I can buy groceries and other basics. But beyond that, I have to ask his permission to have money. He monitors the miles I drive and the calls I make. He has also threatened that if I ever leave him, our teenage kids will stay with him because he controls their "fun" money and savings for their college. In public, everything is "just fine." At home, I'm scared.

Know what you are signing.

- If you ever have a concern or question and your spouse replies, "Don't worry your pretty little head about this, I'll take care of things," this is a red flag. And it's exactly when you need more information. Building trust doesn't happen through ignorance but through respectful learning and sharing.

Keeping someone in the dark, insecure, and unstable is being controlled by another. As psychologist Dr. Bev Smallwood, a member of my mastermind group and author of *This Wasn't Supposed to Happen to Me: 10 Make-or-Break Choices When Life Steals Your Dreams and Rocks Your World* (Thomas Nelson 2009), says, "Manipulative control by deliberately keeping a person uninformed and off balance is emotional abuse."

Knowledge is power; ignorance is not bliss. As women, are we ignorant of important information because we don't ask? Because we don't think we need to know? Because we have fear or distrust of the person who knows? Because we aren't included in the knowing? And do we share the important information from our realm? After all, control can go both ways.

Insights from Our Sisters in Agriculture

- The very best financial advisors I've met are those who invite and include spouses in the discussions and meetings.

- When there's a farm business meeting with our accountant, I'm there. The rest of the farm team and our advisor need to know I'm part of the finances of the farm.

- When my spouse ignores my questions or doesn't share the farm financial reports, I remind him, "I sign loans, I work off the farm to support our personal income so the farm can keep your expenses of salary and health insurance low, and I work on the farm to help as much as I can. So why exactly am I excluded?"

- We wanted our children to grow up knowing the financial realities of the farm business. So, once each of our children turned 10 years old, we called them to the kitchen table once a month for "bill paying night." We had them write out the payee and the amount due, then we adults signed the check. Many times they had questions and we

explained what was happening. Did that make a difference? You bet! One day my husband was filling the corn planter with a bag of seed. Our son who was nearby shouted, "Dad! Don't you dare spill anything. You know how much that bag of seed costs!"

- When I was giving visitors their "first time ever on a farm" tour, they expressed awe of the big machinery and the multitude of shop tools. We walked through the barns and the grain elevator drying and storage areas. Then I heard one of them exclaim, "Man, farmers are rich!" Then it hit me. They actually think we "own" all of this. It was time to talk about Farm Credit and our local bank to give them the full picture.

- Our children didn't receive an allowance. Instead we posted two lists of age-appropriate jobs on our refrigerator. The first was "chores" and there was no pay for them: completing homework, cleaning rooms, picking up toys, doing the dishes, clearing the snow from the walks, taking out the garbage, or feeding the dog. The second list included age-appropriate jobs with a monetary amount attached. For example:

mowing and trimming the farmstead and lawn, cleaning out the mower= $25; sweeping the grain elevator =$5; cleaning the shop = $10; washing the pickup = $5. Their work had to meet our standards. But the money education didn't stop there. We told our children, "Of the money you earned, this part you get to tithe, this part you get to spend, this part you get to save and this part you get to do a surprise for someone. They won't even know it came from you." Our purpose was to teach the joy and responsibility of giving, saving, spending wisely, and showing compassion.

Cathy's Experience

When our children were old enough to power wash and do hog chores, we paid them an hourly wage. They had to fill out a time card and turn it in to get paid. Although they could keep some of their money to spend as they wish, the rest had to be put into the bank for savings.

There's a problem in any family business when a bookkeeper "keeps" the books and no one else has any idea of the system. For those in family businesses, their best interest is met if the data, recordkeeping, and reporting are accurate, timely, and transparent.

Don't keep the "books" to yourself.

Accuracy includes using compatible software for preciseness (not estimates); for details and documentation; for generating reports (e.g., cash flow and net worth statements); benchmark analysis using key ratios; and tax information.

Timely includes updating and entering the data in a timely manner that matches the needs of the business. Do the advisors, owners, and managers want information weekly, monthly, quarterly, semi-annually, annually? Timely also includes paying others without incurring penalties and making sure the farm gets paid on time.

Transparency includes knowing the basics of the financial systems of the business by more than one person, the bookkeeper. Transparency is a form of checks and balances. Ask, "Who could do this work if your bookkeeper wasn't there?"

Jolene's Experience

After one of my workshops, a Sister in Agriculture shared, "Several of my friends and my family had urged me to visit my family doctor. They noticed that during the past months, I wasn't acting like my usual self. I was moody, unfocused, negative, and impatient. So I finally listened. My doctor sent me to the hospital for tests. The MRI showed a massive brain tumor! By the grace of God, my surgery succeeded and the tumor wasn't malignant. During the months before surgery, as sole bookkeeper of the farm business, I believed I had kept up the books as usual. But we discovered I had not been depositing all checks, I'd double-paid some bills, and I'd neglected a few bills that were long overdue. I had also

ignored reminders from our vendors. The lesson? More than one person needs to keep 'eyes' on the books. This is a vital area of the business that requires overview by others."

Insights from Our Sisters in Agriculture

- The farm carries a life insurance policy on my husband, the leader, manager, and head laborer of our business. If he died, we would need to pay somebody as well as advisors to carry that responsibility. Knowing we have that in place gives me peace of mind.

- Each year, the bookkeeper gives an employee compensation report to the leaders and owners of the business. This report specifies what each employee "costs" the business. The compensation total includes salary and all fringe benefits such as housing, insurance, technology, meals, and so on. So many times, those who work on a farm (including a marriage partner) think they get paid "so little." By the time you add up all fringe benefits, though, sometimes "so little" is not "that little."

Insurance equals assurance.

- Before we spend money on farm purchases, we ask, "Will this purchase be an investment to help with income production or is it something we want? Can we afford it or should we do without?"

- Sometimes an investment in one's home is as important to productivity as a piece of equipment.

- Determine how much money is available before making a team decision about how to spend it.

- Being the bookkeeper of the farm business grants me power because I'm in the "know" and others need to learn what I know.

- I only allow so many pieces of new equipment to go by my kitchen window before I start asking questions.

- I'm the bookkeeper for the farm. My problem is that no one else in the family business is interested in learning this work. Things would be in a real mess if I didn't show up. We need a Plan B.

- You have no idea how great we felt when we saw PAID IN FULL stamped on the front on our Farm Credit loan document. Those three words could have also read RELIEF. PRIDE. JOY.

Family counselors know that money is one of the most common reasons couples argue. And in agriculture, the phrase "for richer, for poorer" covers the spectrum most farmers experience.

To ride the roller coaster of markets, income, and expenses, debt and repayment, you need a strong spine and a sharp mind. Understand the facts of money in both your business and your personal life. You need this to lead, manage, and support the farm and your family, too. ❖

CHAPTER 11

"In sickness and in health."

REST AND RECREATION ESSENTIALS

We balance soil fertility, feed rations, truck tires, and checkbooks. We overwork, overwhelm, and overload ourselves. Something's wrong with this picture! Creating a time to renew ourselves allows us to be our best—and give our best to others. The challenge we have in agriculture is that we live where we work, and we work where we live. So we actually have to vacate to have a vacation.

Jolene's Experience

During my workshop The Balancing Act, I ask attendees to recall the growing-up memories of their vacations. The room fills with the buzz of crazy road trips, camping in canvas tents, first airplane rides, visits to see family far away, and state fair adventures. Yet I couldn't help but notice three women sitting in silence—a mom with silent tears rolling down her cheeks and her two adult daughters looking down, staring at their handouts. When I approached them, the mom shared, "We have nothing to talk about because we never took a vacation. We milked cows twice a day, every day. We celebrated the birth of their calves, the increase in milk to sell, the new dairy barn. But we never celebrated ourselves."

Then I watched as her spine straightened. She wiped her eyes and while looking at her adult daughters said, "Get ready. I'm about to spend some of your inheritance. We're all going to Disney World—you, me, Dad, your husbands, and all the kids. Let's look right now look at our calendars. What week would work best?" And she made it happen! She sent me a Mickey Mouse postcard from Florida. The only thing on the back was a huge smiley face and her signature.

Cathy's Experience

Parents often think they need to take their children on elaborate vacations. I used to be one of those parents—until my children proved to me I did not.

Our two boys were in elementary school when we took them on a "real" vacation. In previous years, we had taken the boys fishing to the lake my husband had fished on as a young child. Both boys had inherited a love for fishing from him.

Vacate for a vacation.

One evening, we cornered each boy separately (so that neither brother would be influenced by the other) to ask them to choose what to do for our next vacation. Because they were history buffs, we proposed two history destinations: Mount Rushmore /Black Hills and our nation's capital, Washington, DC. We also gave them the option of returning to

the fishing resort from vacations past. Both my husband and I made a big deal out of the first two options, pointing out how much fun we'd have visiting either destination. We only briefly mentioned the option of fishing. We couldn't believe it when both boys emphatically chose to go fishing. Our youngest son exclaimed, "You mean we get to go fishing AGAIN? I just can't believe it!"

It shows you that most kids really don't care where they go; they just care that you go somewhere. Our somewhere for them was to go fishing—always.

Insights from Our Sisters in Agriculture

- We couldn't believe it! We were gone from the farm for seven nights in a row, and when we returned, the farm was still there!

- I often chuckle that people in Canada take a holiday and celebrate. In America, we take a vacation and feel guilty. There's a lesson to be learned from our neighbors to the north.

> Don't feel guilty for going on a vacation!

- Buy nonrefundable airline tickets. That way he can't start chopping days off "the getaway" as time goes on.

- A wedding gift from my husband's parents was three days of time off for a honeymoon to the Farm Progress Show. And we did have a good time, but we didn't tell them how much of that time we really spent at the Show!

- When the car is the method of travel for our vacation, it finds its way to the driveways of implement dealerships on our journey. After a few of those stops, I learned to slip into the driver's seat so that same car finds its way to some cute antique shops. A woman's gotta do what a woman's gotta do.

- Who said you can only take a vacation with your husband, especially

if you can't get your husband to go? Instead, I plan vacations with my girlfriends, and when I return, I often find I'm more appreciated than ever. Sometimes I come home and the family has accomplished things that surprise me. Last time, I drove up to my house after being gone and noticed my husband had installed new windows! True story.

- Be prepared. Once you set a departure date for vacation, the animals will get out and the basement freezer will quit working. Be ready. Plan B is needed so you can continue with Plan A.

- I'd been having a few tough months dealing with life's situations. My husband, known best as Grandpa, decided this Grandma needed a vacation. So he made plans and we packed up. As we were saying our goodbyes to our kids and grandkids, our youngest grandson quipped, "Grandpa! Don't bring Grandma back unless she has an attitude adjustment!" Funny how my grandson knew what I needed and I didn't.

Research shows there is great value to a business and individuals when we schedule and actually take a break. We all need something to look forward to—an escape, a new environment, a time away from the farm to broaden our perspective, learn new things, celebrate old or new joys, renew relationships, and restore our energy.

Jolene's Advice

Expect immediate and concrete benefits for both the household and farmstead the minute "Vacation" is written on the calendar, including these:

- **Increased creativity**—When we put ourselves in a different environment, we allow our brains to think differently. Creativity and innovation replace the rut of same place, same responsibility. To "think outside of the box," it's helpful to "get outside of the box."

We all need something to look forward to.

- **Increased productivity**—Now that you have a deadline declaring a break from the job, you'll be more efficient, organized, and focused on the tasks at hand. Also, since the whole work team knows in advance you'll be gone, they focus as well. They don't want to do all of your work while you're gone.

- **Stronger relationships**—Spouses and children need to know you value a few days with them as much as you value the farm. Their smiles start the minute you mark "Vacation" on the calendar and widen as plans are made. Anticipation builds. A time away is a gift to them and to you. The results are happier marriages and better parenting.

- **Better health**—A good antidote to burned out, stressed out, and worn out is rest, relax, and renew. Don't plan a vacation with lists of "to do" for every minute. Instead, enjoy the highlights with a slower pace and open eyes. You just may find yourself breathing deeply with a slower heart rate. Healthier people make for healthier businesses and happier times for all around.

And one last thing. Don't forget, many women have in our DNA that before we leave on a vacation, we must clean the house. Heaven forbid something happens to us and our relatives walk into a messy house! ❖

CHAPTER 12

"Till death do us part."

LEFT BEHIND BUT NOT ALONE

One of the joys of working with our Sisters in Agriculture is observing and learning from the experience of multiple generations. But widowhood can happen at any stage in life.

Jolene's Experience

Although I've not walked the path of widowhood, I've become a student of those who have.

At a Women in Ag conference, I invited three special women to serve on a panel. Each had recently lost a spouse. As I prepared them for the session, I thanked them for their vulnerability, strength, and willingness to share. Then I explained, "I will only be asking you three questions:

1.) If you had one more day, what would you do?

2.) If you had one more day, what would you ask?

3.) If you had one more day, what would you say?"

That day, we laughed, we cried, and we laughed so hard we cried.

For example, we learned:

- When a man is the widow, everyone continually brings him food; when a female is the widow, you'll get food the day of the funeral. Then you're on your own.

- I never knew I could cry so hard or so often.

- I learned that wills can be changed on a whim. And if at the time of dating and signing a will, the testator is of sound mind, it stands. What is legal is legal. I had no idea my husband had changed his will until he died.

  I never knew I could cry so hard or so often.

- A buy-sell agreement and long-term contracts are more important than a will. Be sure your documents are current, include specific information for terms, and do what you want them to do. Those documents can be your security and assure the business might continue.

- Ask for names: Who's the plumber, the electrician, the repairman? Who does maintenance for the well and the air/heating system? Who are the advisors for marketing, crop and livestock information, insurance, accounting, tax prep, legal work? Who do you trust to help me?

- The second year is harder than the first. The first year, you are in a fog of grief, but you're kept busy doing what has to be done (settling the estate, meeting with advisors, learning your new role in the business and family, establishing some kind of a new routine). Then the busyness of the first year ends. You no longer meet frequently with advisors, neighbors, family, and friends. You have more time to think, remember, and grieve. And you realize you are really alone.

- Know that the easy days ahead will be easy; the hard days will be hard. Sometimes it is doing nothing or only little things during those tough times that let you survive.

- After time had passed, a few single farmers stop by to visit and some to ask me out. I didn't know if they were interested in me for me or it they wanted my land.

- I had to forgive myself. I know it doesn't make sense, but I had a lot of "if only I had done ____, this wouldn't have happened." The weight of guilt on my shoulders seemed unbearable. With a help of a counselor I realized that not everything that happens to me happens because of me. What a relief to change from the weight of "if only" guilt to only feeling sadness or gladness and figuring out what I can do going forward.

Keep a gratitude journal.

- The key to my journey as a new widow was the pad of paper I kept by my night stand. Each evening I added a new entry of three things for which I was grateful. It allowed me to close my eyes thinking about something cheerful.

One week after the panel, I received a letter from one of the attendees who wrote, "It's been a year since my husband died and I'm still mad. Mad at him because he never explained things and left me with a real mess, and mad at myself for not asking questions. I couldn't even grieve and remember the special times. Instead, I was just so overwhelmed and fearful. Nothing had ever been explained: the books, the contracts, the assets, the debts. I became physically ill, made stupid decisions, and sold it all. So please, tell people to get their business in order now. Ask questions. Write things down. Don't wait."

Insights from Our Sisters in Agriculture

- Maturity doesn't come with age; it comes with accepting responsibility for the reality that has been made.

- Wills are individual documents. You do not have to wait for your spouse to create your will. Make a list of properties/assets owned and document how things are titled. What would be included in your estate? Tell your spouse the date you are going to the attorney to create or revise your will. Believe me, he'll want to come too. He wants to know your distribution plan. Most often, your spouse will work on his will at the same time as you.

- When you need help, your friends, family, and faith will carry you. But you must be vulnerable enough to ask for help.

- If your spouse has named you the executor of his will and his power of attorney for finances and health care, you may need to know a heck of a lot more than you do now. Ask him questions while you can. Observe the workings of the business with different eyes knowing you will be responsible.

- Right now, become informed regarding everyone your farm does business with. I was astounded when, after my husband and farm leader was killed, I received thousands of dollars of invoices from people I didn't know. Yet these invoices didn't make sense as expenses on our farm. I discovered they came from crooks preying on new widows.

- Everyone advises a newly widowed woman on the farm to sell out and move to town. Do not, repeat: do NOT sell out until you are ready to do so. And don't make major decisions in the first 12 months.

Purchase life insurance policies on each of your key farm partners right away and have a legal buy-sell agreement. That way you can hire the right and responsible person to work with you. Also, you'll have the necessary money to buy out heirs so you can keep on farming or keep the farm intact for your heirs.

• When someone dies, property is transferred three ways: gifting, buying, and pilfering. Things often disappear from the house and business when someone dies. Be ready.

Jolene's Experience

It's so important to learn from others who have been on the journey of widowhood. After listening to my Sisters in Agriculture, I, too, had much to do. So, on a long car drive, I informed my husband, "Honey, there will be no radio today. No markets. No weather. No talk show host. It's just you and me and a legal size pad of paper. I have an important question for you. What do you want done with your body when you're dead?" How's that for a conversation starter?

Ask the tough questions now.

What followed were oodles of questions, lots of notes, tons of valuable insight. On the way home, I drove and he asked me the same questions. Fourteen pages later we had a list of "details for those left behind." Doing this was truly a tribute to life and living, not death.

The time will come when you realize you get to start over and create the life you want for yourself from here on out. You will experience a different life and a kind of freedom empowered with choices to make—for you.

As one woman shared, "I was left behind, but I was not alone." She was walking on her path one day at a time, reaching out as she needed, but learning to live a different life. ❖

CHAPTER 13

"And I'm to know that...how?"

FINAL THOUGHTS FROM THE FARM

The sentiments in this book have brought all kinds of eye-opening moments, treasured memories, and times of pure joy and laughter. Know this: just about the time you think you know the "rules of the game," you realize more lessons must still be learned from our Sisters in Agriculture.

Here are a few more lessons!

Insights from Our Sisters in Agriculture

- Get thick skin. Feelings and egos can be easily bruised, especially when nights are short and days are long. Remembering why you do what you do will help you through the tough times. Having your reasons written down is even more helpful.

- Don't be afraid to ask your neighbors or any woman in business multiple questions and listen for her answers. She may be your best teacher.

- We have a policy on our family farm: Only one person on the team can be crabby at a time—and it's not your turn!

- I baked a large ham in my roaster and served it whole, to be sliced at the table. When my husband asked why I didn't cut off the ends before serving it like his mom always did, I replied, "I have a bigger roasting pan than she does. She has to cut off the ends so it will fit into her pan. Next question?"

- It's important to know why you married that man. Reminding yourself helps you overcome all the reasons you want to kill him.

- Be ready for friends and family to not understand your world. And it's OK if you don't immediately understand "ag speak," its acronyms and analogies. Those of us involved in agriculture our entire lives still have moments of not understanding a conversation. Just remember, you are not alone!

- As a farmer, a strong will and strong body are needed. The farm doesn't care if you are younger or older, starting out or experienced, wealthy or struggling. Even with all the technological advances of today, you need a strong body too. There is only so much a computer and mechanization can do.

- Sometimes the only thing I can do is pray. But it's also the most important thing I can do.

I wouldn't trade farm life for anything.

- To be able to live life on the farm is not easy, but I wouldn't trade it for anything. Nothing turns me on more than to watch my husband work in the fields. He's my tractor stud. Love grows deeper on the farm.

- I married my farmer in April. Our first anniversary was spent hauling manure, but our 25th anniversary was an extended trip to Alaska. Don't be afraid to marry a farmer, even in April.

- If all else fails, remember, "If he didn't see it, it never happened!" and "What they don't know won't hurt them!"

- My husband always tells our two daughters, "You will never find a husband like your mom did." I say, "Good Lord, I hope not." I guess he's not that bad. I just like to give him crap back.

———————————

One thing we know, there's nothing better and more challenging than being married to a farmer, one who is connected to the land, equipment, plants, and animals. And we know there is nothing more important than faith, family, and friends. When all are combined, we work hard, laugh lots, shed tears, find support, learn lessons, and celebrate our blessings. Being married to a farmer requires lots of collaboration and negotiation to traverse the terrain.

But most of all, we know it requires perspective and a great sense of humor. That's why we are thankful for our Sisters in Agriculture. They've been there and done that. They explain or expand our vision. They ask questions and open eyes. They provide caring hearts and joy-filled, enduring spirits. They make us laugh and chuckle, and sometimes we even think, "I'm so glad that happened to you and not to me."

I hope you've found the wisdom in this book both insightful and fun. Most of all, know that if you've married a farmer, you don't need to walk the years alone. You'll find more than hope from your Sisters in Agriculture; you'll find help and humor!

Let's enjoy the ride—together! Jolene

Acknowledgments

So many have encouraged the writing of this book with their support, laughs, tears, and cheers.

To my real Farmer Brown, Keith: For more than four decades, you have given me the gift of a loving man and a working farm. You've also been the "teacher" behind many of my insights and a non-stop source of testing my mettle of being married to a farmer.

To Cathy Riley: Thanks for being my friend and a major contributor to this book. Your husband, Mike, also earns my thanks for his role in contributing to your many insightful stories.

To Carolyn Harold, office manager extraordinaire: You are there every time I needed a word. Your steadfast devotion to this book has greatly aided in the result.

To Barbara McNichol, editor: You helped make sense out of the pieces and led the way to improving this book's readability. My many thanks to you and your talents.

To the book designer, Matthew, and book illustrator, Chuck: Your creativity is beyond measure. You bring character to the moments and memories.

To our Sisters in Agriculture: This book wouldn't exist without you, your experience, and your support. It was your vulnerability, solutions, and humor that had us all giggling and sharing stories.

All of your contributions have reaffirmed the amazing value you bring to the agricultural world we live in. Thanks for your valuable insights that have brought bountiful fun and ah-ha moments to this book.

About the Author

Jolene Brown is a walking-talking spokesperson and champion for the people of agriculture. This farmer, author, professional speaker, and family business consultant is on a mission to share best practices, appreciation, laughter, and celebration. Jolene's worldwide audiences appreciate her fun-filled spirit and valuable information.

Jolene's book, *Sometimes You Need More Than a 2x4! How-to-tips to successfully grow a family business*, is in its fourth printing. Her writings for the Successful Farming magazine column "Can Their Problem Be Solved?" are read by thousands. She also blogs for PinkTractor.com, a website for Women in Agriculture.

This Iowa-based speaker is an award winning communicator and an honored recipient of the Certified Speaking Professional, the highest earned designation of speaking achievement from the National Speakers Association! She has also received the esteemed Legend of the Speaking Profession award from her peers in the speaking profession.

But above all, Jolene is a real Farmer Brown. Her greatest claim to fame is still being married—even though she's dented the grain bin, plugged the augers, and provided levity to people at the equipment parts counters.

Visit her website at **www.JoleneBrown.com**

P.S. I'd love to hear from you. If you have insightful, fun stories to share, please email them to me at Jolene@JoleneBrown.com

CPSIA information can be obtained
at www.ICGtesting.com
Printed in the USA
LVOW01s0329110217
523929LV00003B/5/P

9 781945 330513